DK POCKET EYEWITNESS

SHARKS

FACTS AT YOUR FINGERTIPS

DK INDIA
Project editor Virien Chopra
Project art editor Nishesh Batnagar
Senior editor Kingshuk Ghoshal
Senior art editor Govind Mittal
Editors Rashmi Rajan, Jubbi Francis
Assistant art editor Tanya Mehrotra
Jacket designer Juhi Sheth
Jackets editorial coordinator Priyanka Sharma
DTP designers Dheeraj Arora, Jaypal Singh
Picture researcher Sumedha Chopra
Managing editor Saloni Talwar
Managing art editor Romi Chakraborty
CTS manager Balwant Singh
Production manager Pankaj Sharma

DK LONDON
Senior editor Fleur Star
Senior art editor Philip Letsu
Jacket designer Surabhi Wadhwa-Gandhi
Jacket editor Amelia Collins
Jacket design development manager Sophia MTT
Production editor Ben Marcus
Production controller Mary Slater

Publisher Andrew Macintyre
Associate publishing director Liz Wheeler
Art director Phil Ormerod
Publishing director Jonathan Metcalf

Consultant Dr Trevor Day

This edition published in 2018
First published in Great Britain in 2012 by Dorling Kindersley Limited
20 Vauxhall Bridge Road,
London SW1V 2SA

The authorised representative in the EEA is
Dorling Kindersley Verlag GmbH. Arnulfstr. 124,
80636 Munich, Germany

15 14 13 12 11 10 9
009–310512–Oct/2018

A CIP catalogue record for this book
is available from the British Library.
ISBN: 978-0-2413-4361-6

Printed and bound in China

www.dk.com

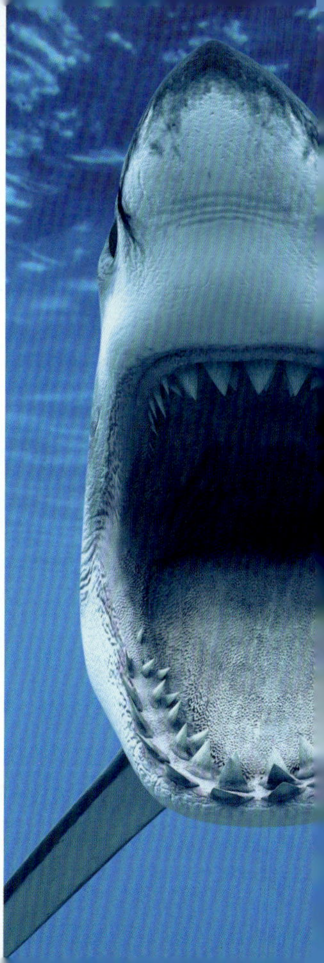

CONTENTS

Scales and sizes
This book contains profiles of sharks, rays, skates, and chimaeras with scale drawings to indicate their size.

1.8 m (6 ft)

20 cm (8 in)

Endangered sharks
This label indicates that the fish is endangered or critically endangered.

ENDANGERED

The shark

Sharks are cartilaginous fish, meaning they have a skeleton made of cartilage, a lighter and more flexible substance than bone. Millions of years of evolution have made sharks some of the deadliest predators in the oceans. Excellent eyesight, powerful jaws, and a streamlined body make them efficient and dominant hunters.

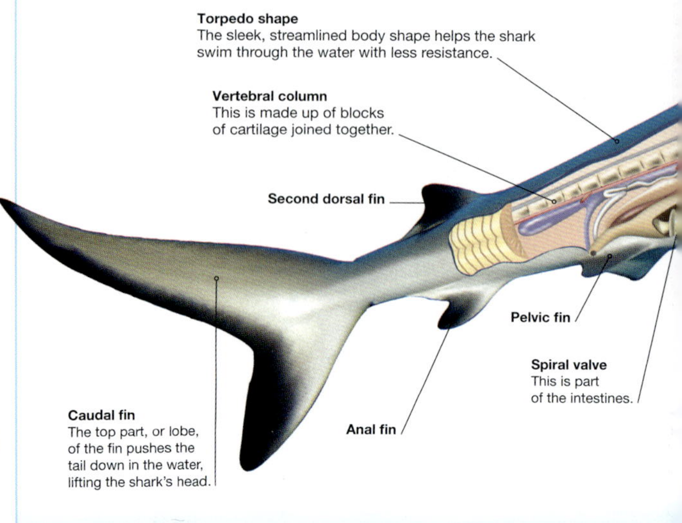

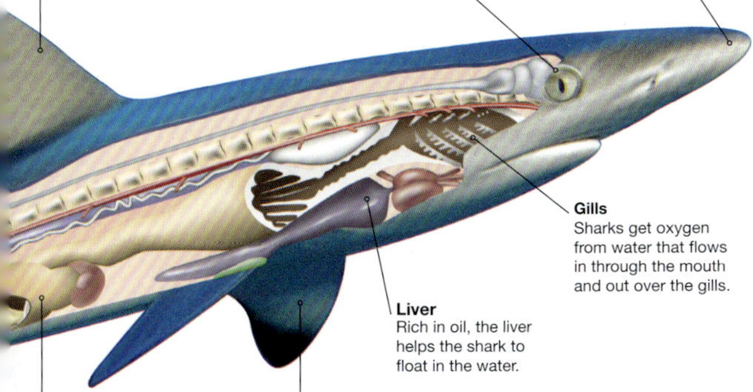

Eye
All sharks have good eyesight. Some have a protective, transparent covering over their eyes called the nictitating membrane.

Ampullae of Lorenzini
These small pores on the snout pick up electrical signals given off by potential prey.

First dorsal fin
The dorsal, anal, and pelvic fins stop the shark rolling over.

Gills
Sharks get oxygen from water that flows in through the mouth and out over the gills.

Liver
Rich in oil, the liver helps the shark to float in the water.

Stomach
The U-shaped stomach can turn inside-out to regurgitate a meal.

Pectoral fin
This pair of fins steers and gives lift.

-teral line

harks, like other fish, have line of special cells along e length of their body. This ne detects vibrations in the water, ich as the movements of potential prey.

Brownbanded bambooshark

Lateral line
The white line on this image follows the actual lateral line of this shark.

Making sense

Sharks have superb senses that allow them to be among the top predators on the planet. Apart from the five senses they share with people – sight, touch, taste, hearing, and smell – sharks also have an electrical sense that helps them locate prey.

Ampullae of Lorenzini appear as dark spots on snout

Mako shark

Electrical sense

All living things give off electrical signals. Sharks have special organs called the ampullae of Lorenzini that detect such signals to help them find prey at close range. The ampullae are a network of thousands of pores on a shark's snout. The pores pick up the signals and transmit them to the shark's brain, helping it pinpoint the prey's location.

Barbels

Some sharks that live near the sea bed have sensitive, whiskerlike organs called barbels that help them "taste" and "smell" chemicals given off by prey. Dragging the barbels over the sea bed allows them to pick up vibrations in the sand made by buried sea animals.

Barbel on a nurse shark

Eye of a scalloped hammerhead shark

All-round vision

Most sharks can see well even in dim light. Hammerhead sharks have another advantage. Their eyes point sideways and are placed on the ends of the narrow blades of its head. This gives them a large field of vision, letting them see in all directions at once.

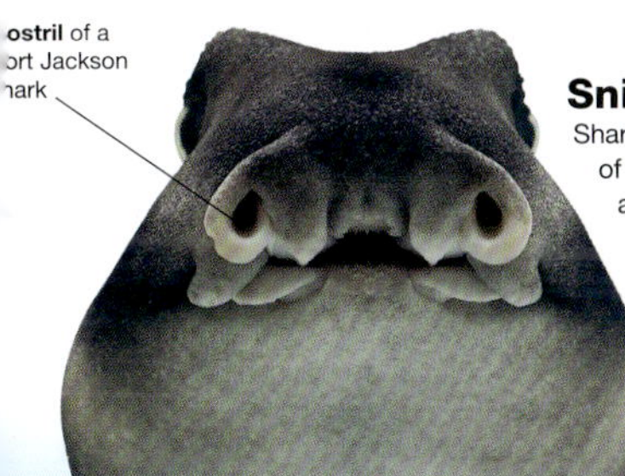

ostril of a ort Jackson hark

Sniffing out

Sharks have a highly developed sense of smell. Some species can detect a drop of blood in the water from hundreds of metres away. A shark can tell the direction of its prey as soon as one of its nostrils detects the scent, in the same way our ears tell us where sound is coming from.

Teeth and jaws

Shark teeth come in different shapes and sizes and have different uses. Long, curved teeth help to get hold of slippery fish, while serrated (sawlike) teeth are used to bite off chunks of prey. Some sharks have tiny teeth that strain food from the water, while others have flat teeth to crush hard-shelled prey.

Basking sharks can have up to 1,500 teeth, but no one knows what they use them for

No chewing

Basking sharks and megamouth sharks are two of the largest species, but they fill up on the smallest prey – tiny creatures called plankton. These sharks are filter feeders, which means they do not use their teeth to feed. Instead, they strain plankton from the water with comblike structures in their gill slits.

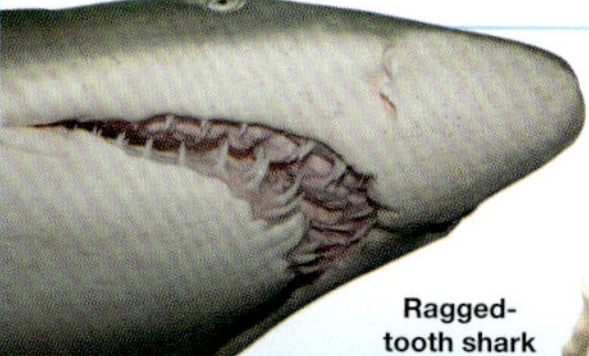

Ragged-tooth shark

Sharp as a needle

Sharks that feed on slippery fish and squid need to be able to hold on to their prey. The long, pointed teeth of these sharks grip the prey's body, preventing it from escaping.

Port Jackson **shark** with open mouth showing flat teeth

A lot to eat

A shark's jaws are connected ery loosely to its skull, allowing the shark to push out its jaws and take a big bite. Multiple ows of sharp teeth ensure that the prey does not get away.

Breaking through

Some sharks feed on crabs, mussels, and other shellfish. To get past the prey's protective shell, these sharks have flat teeth at the back of their jaws that grind together, crushing the hard outer covering.

Great white shark

Tiger shark tooth and jaws

Double-edged saw

Sharks that prey on seals and other sea mammals have triangular teeth that are serrated like a saw on two sides. They use these to rip pieces of flesh from the prey.

Swimming

Sharks are some of the fastest swimmers in the ocean. They propel themselves through water by moving their tails from side to side. Swimming not only helps a shark to catch prey, but also moves water over its gills, allowing it to breathe.

S is for swimming

As a shark swims, its body curves in an S-shape, pushing itself forward. It uses its pectoral fins to provide lift and change direction. It cannot flap its fins, but by making small changes to the angle of the fins, it can move up, down, left, and right.

1. Muscles in the body contract, making the head curve to one side.

Smallspotted catshark

2. The curve moves t the middle of the bod as the head move to the other side

Step by step

Some sharks that live near coral reefs or on the sea bed use their pectoral fins not only for swimming but for walking as well. These sharks pu themselves along with their fins while the search the ree or sea be for food

Epaulette shar

‹wim or die

harks breathe by using their gills to draw oxygen om the water. Most sharks are able to pump ater over their gills by swallowing water as ey swim. However, some sharks, ıch as the mako shark, have st this ability and must eep swimming ɔ that water is ɔntinuously assing over eir gills.

xygen pump

ɔme sharks that live on the ocean ɔor do not move around much. To ɜt oxygen, they take in water through two bes called spiracles. Muscular movements aw in water through the spiracles, and ıss it over the gills that are located ı the underside of the body.

Reproduction

Sharks produce pups in three ways. Some lay eggs – they are oviparous. Some give birth to live young – they are viviparous. But most are both – they are ovoviviparous, which means the young develop inside eggs but hatch while they are still inside their mother.

Inside an egg

Oviparous sharks lay their eggs in the water, where they are in constant danger of being swept away. To prevent this, the eggs of some species, such as catsharks, have tendrils that wrap around seaweed, anchoring the eggs while the baby shark grows inside.

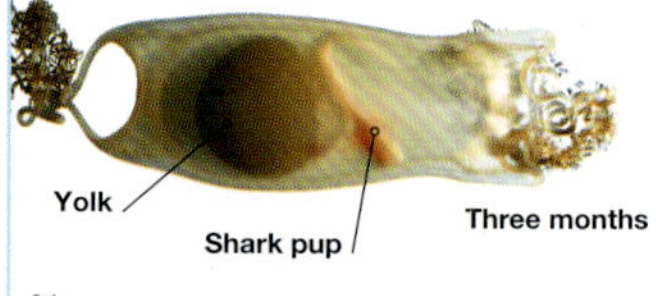

1. Inside the egg of this smallspotted catshark, the embryo starts to form. It is attached to a yolk sac, from which it draws nourishment.

2. As the embryo grows and uses up the nourishment, the yolk sac shrinks. Water seeps into the egg, providing oxygen to the embryo.

3. Eight to nine months after the egg is laid, the young catshark, called a pup, hatches and swims out into the sea.

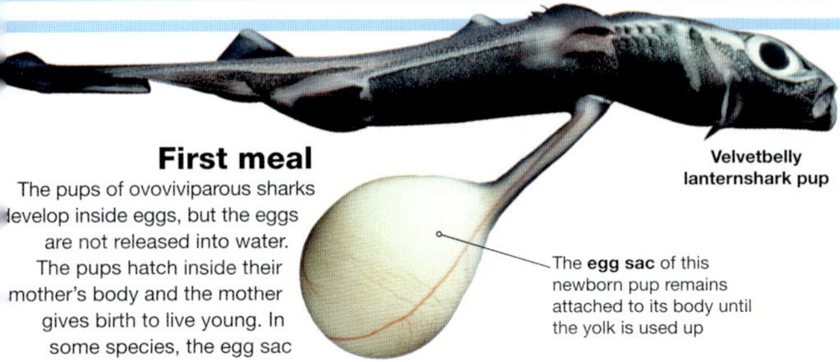

First meal

The pups of ovoviviparous sharks develop inside eggs, but the eggs are not released into water. The pups hatch inside their mother's body and the mother gives birth to live young. In some species, the egg sac remains connected to the pup after birth, providing its first meal.

Velvetbelly lanternshark pup

The **egg sac** of this newborn pup remains attached to its body until the yolk is used up

Newly born **lemon shark** pup with umbilical cord still attached

Growing inside

In viviparous sharks, the young grow inside the mother, and get both nourishment and oxygen from her through a tube called the umbilical cord. Once the embryos are ready to be born, the mother heads for shallow waters to give birth.

Attack and defence

Speed, strength, and agility make sharks some of the deadliest predators on the planet. Different species of shark hunt in different ways. Some chase down their prey, while others hide and wait before ambushing their prey.

Pelagic thresher shark

The thresher's tail

Certain species of thresher shark use their long tails and speed to hunt prey. Swimming around a school of fish, the thresher herds them into a small area with its tail. Once the fish are packed together tightly, the shark swoops in and grabs one in its teeth.

Fast hunters

Big sharks such as makos and great whites rely on their speed to catch prey. They have been recorded chasing after seals and other prey at more than 40 kph (25 mph). They go so fast that they can leap out of the water completely.

Great white catching a seal

Mistaken identity

On rare occasions, sharks can attack humans. However, this is most likely to occur when they mistake us for their normal prey. For example, to a shark, a surfer looks a lot like a swimming seal.

Surfer on board

Seal

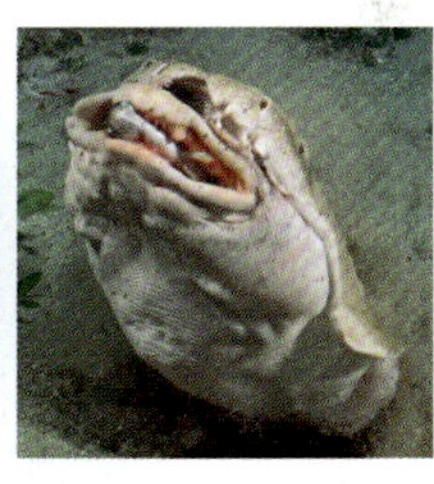

Ambush

Some sharks, such as angelsharks, which live near the sea bed have evolved a particularly effective way to catch prey. They hide themselves in the sand and wait for fish to swim by. Once a fish is close enough, they strike fast.

Shark hunters

Sharks can also be prey themselves. Killer whales, or orcas, sometimes hunt sharks, including makos and great white sharks. The only defence these sharks have against the orcas is to use their speed and agility to escape.

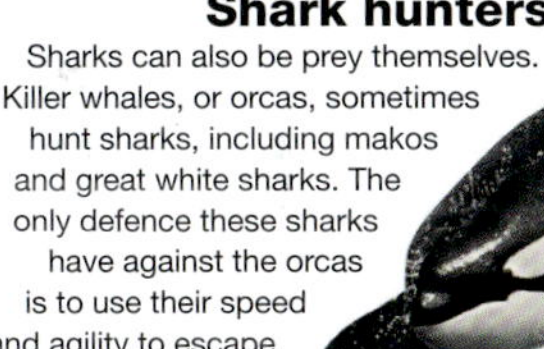

Orca

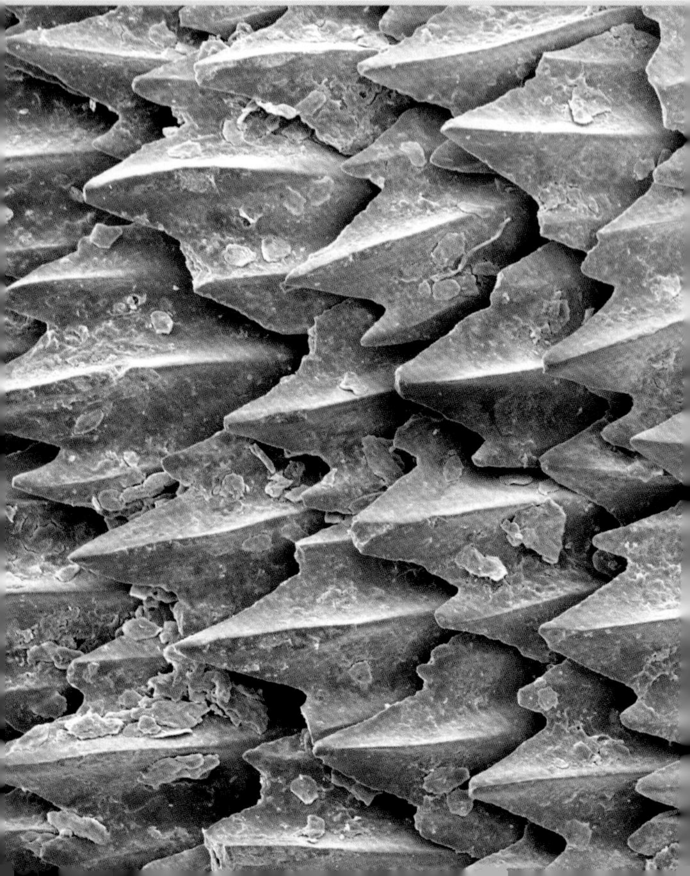

A shark's scales are like teeth: soft inside with a hard, enamel-like coating

DENTICLES

A shark's body is covered in small scales called denticles that act as protective armour against injuries. They also help to make the shark more streamlined so it can swim faster.

Habitats

Sharks live in every ocean in the world, and a few species even live in rivers. Some ocean-dwelling sharks move between warm and cool seas, but most are adapted to a particular kind of habitat, from shallow coastal waters to deep, open water.

Shark homes

Sharks live in different parts of the ocean at varying distances from land: coastal waters, continental shelves, slopes, and open water. Many coastal sharks inhabit coral reefs, where food is plentiful. The majority of sharks live in the shallow, food-rich waters above continental shelves or in the deeper waters above continental slopes, where the sea bed drops away. Further out to sea, sharks that live in open water are called pelagic. Many rely on speed to catch prey.

Coral reefs are home to sharks such as the whitetip reef shark.

Coastal waters are home to sharks such as salmon sharks and whitenose sharks.

Shortfin makos live in the open seas, where great whites also spend part of their time.

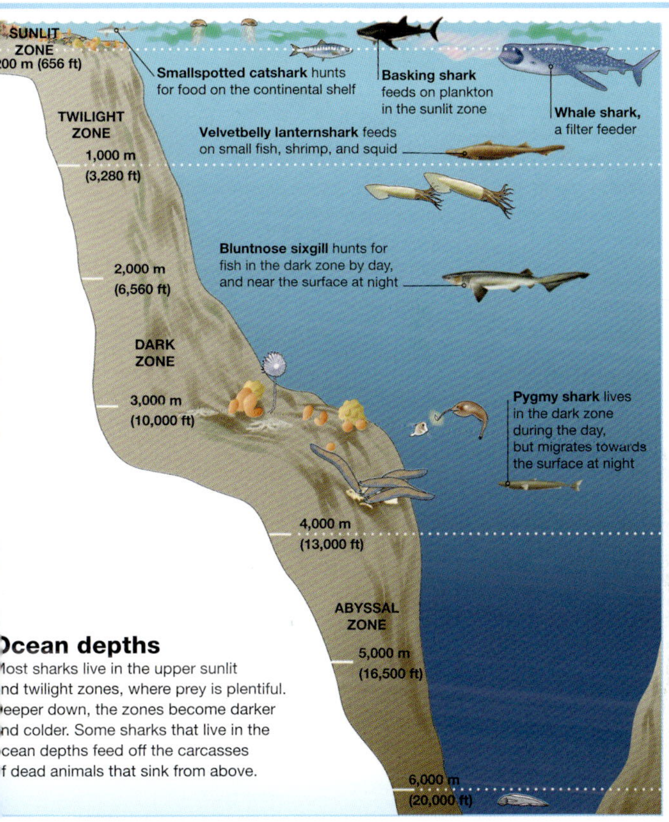

Ocean depths

Most sharks live in the upper sunlit and twilight zones, where prey is plentiful. Deeper down, the zones become darker and colder. Some sharks that live in the ocean depths feed off the carcasses of dead animals that sink from above.

Migration

Many sharks undertake long, regular journeys from one location to another, which is called migration. Different species of shark migrate for different reasons. Sometimes they move to find mates, sometimes to find a safe place to give birth. Some also migrate to the breeding grounds of their prey, where there is plenty of food available.

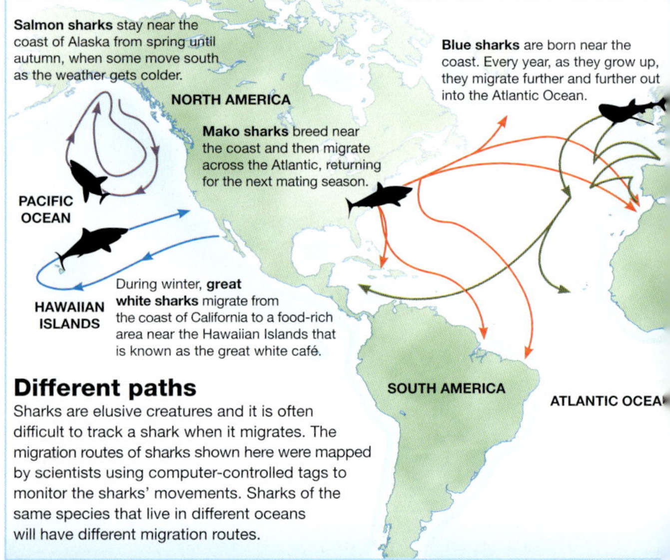

Different paths

Sharks are elusive creatures and it is often difficult to track a shark when it migrates. The migration routes of sharks shown here were mapped by scientists using computer-controlled tags to monitor the sharks' movements. Sharks of the same species that live in different oceans will have different migration routes.

WHY SHARKS MIGRATE

To mate. Sharks migrate to breeding grounds to find mates.

To have pups. Female sharks often migrate to shallow waters to give birth.

For food. Sharks often follow the migration patterns of their prey.

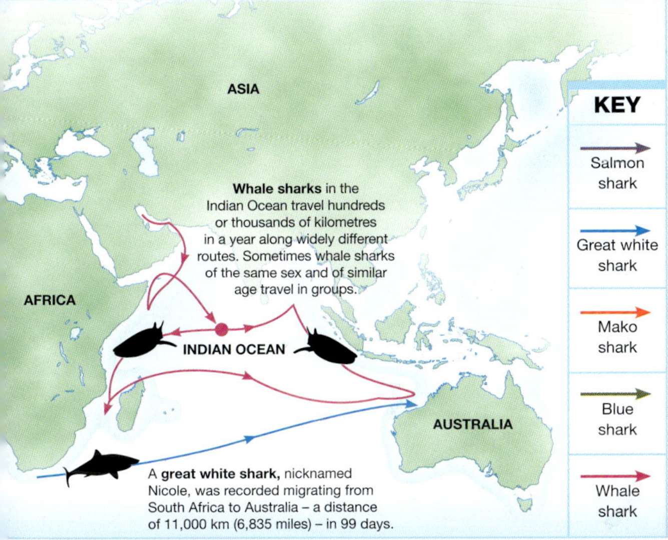

ASIA

AFRICA

INDIAN OCEAN

AUSTRALIA

Whale sharks in the Indian Ocean travel hundreds or thousands of kilometres in a year along widely different routes. Sometimes whale sharks of the same sex and of similar age travel in groups.

A **great white shark,** nicknamed Nicole, was recorded migrating from South Africa to Australia – a distance of 11,000 km (6,835 miles) – in 99 days.

KEY

- Salmon shark
- Great white shark
- Mako shark
- Blue shark
- Whale shark

Sharks under threat

Sharks are hunted by people for their meat, fins, and sometimes just for sport. Many species of shark are endangered and some are at risk of becoming extinct. Efforts are now being made to protect the most endangered species.

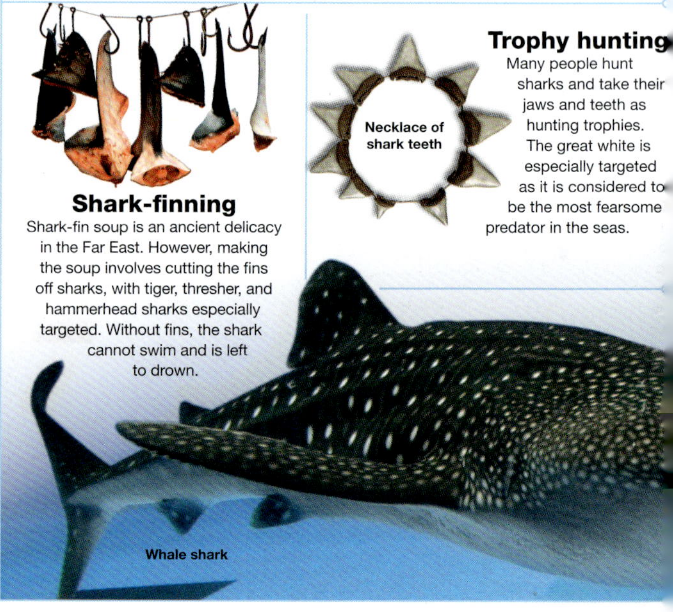

Shark-finning

Shark-fin soup is an ancient delicacy in the Far East. However, making the soup involves cutting the fins off sharks, with tiger, thresher, and hammerhead sharks especially targeted. Without fins, the shark cannot swim and is left to drown.

Necklace of shark teeth

Trophy hunting

Many people hunt sharks and take their jaws and teeth as hunting trophies. The great white is especially targeted as it is considered to be the most fearsome predator in the seas.

Whale shark

Tagging

Protecting sharks is difficult as little is known about most species. To find out more, scientists attach electronic tags to the dorsal fins of sharks in order to monitor their behaviour and movements. Understanding how sharks live helps in creating programmes for their conservation.

Scientist attaching a tag to a Caribbean reef shark

n captivity

ne way to protect endangered shark pecies is to breed them in captivity. owever, most sharks cannot survive r long in aquariums as they need large volume of water that has enough ygen for breathing. Most aquarium sharks are released into the wild after a few months.

Ancient sharks

Fossil evidence shows that sharks have existed for more than 400 million years. The most common type of shark fossils are teeth, because sharks shed many teeth in a lifetime. Some modern sharks are very similar to their ancestors because they have remained successful and have not changed their way of life.

Cladoselache

Although it lived more than 370 million years ago, the shape of this shark had features that resemble both modern frilled sharks and mackerel sharks. However, it did not have any scales on its body, except around the edges of its fins, mouth, and eyes.

SIZE 1.5 m (5 ft)

HABITAT Open oceans

DISTRIBUTION Fossils found in North America and Europe

Hybodus

A prehistoric shark that existed 165 million years ago, *Hybodus* lived in shallow seas across the world. It had two types of teeth – sharp ones ripped into fish and flat ones ground hard-shelled animals, such as molluscs.

SIZE 2.5 m (8.25 ft)

HABITAT Shallow seas

DISTRIBUTION Fossils found in Asia, Europe, Africa, and North America

Megalodon

Megalodon was one of the largest predators ever to have lived. It existed more than 1.5 million years ago and was similar in appearance to the great white shark. This shark could rip away the fins of other fish and crush the shells of giant sea turtles with a single bite.

SIZE 20 m (66 ft)

HABITAT Open oceans

DISTRIBUTION Worldwide

Stethacanthus

Stethacanthus swam the oceans more than 360 million years ago. Its most striking feature was the unusual shape of its dorsal fin. Shaped like an anvil or ironing board, the bulbous shape was found only in males. They probably used it as a prominent feature to attract females for mating.

SIZE 2 m (6.5 ft)

HABITAT Open oceans

DISTRIBUTION Fossils found in North America and Scotland

HELICOPRION
This shark, whose name means "spiral saw", lived around 280 million years ago. The only fossils that have been found are of its whorl of teeth. This reconstruction shows the whorl growing from the front of the snout, but it's more likely to have been inside the mouth.

Helicoprion had a whorl of 180 teeth like a circular saw blade the size of a dinner plate

Sharks

Sharks include the largest fish in the world – and some that are a tiny fraction of that size. There are more than 450 species that range from the dwarf lanternshark, which is a mere 21 cm (8.5 in) long, to the whale shark, which can grow to 18 m (59 ft) long. Sharks are found in every ocean and some rivers. They are all carnivorous, but despite the fearsome reputation of some, including the great white shark (left), many are not dangerous to people.

CARIBBEAN REEF SHARK
Most sharks are active during the day, but the Caribbean reef shark often rests during the day and hunts at night.

Identifying sharks

There are more than 450 species of shark in the world today. The different species are placed in eight groups, or orders, based on particular body features, some of which are shown here.

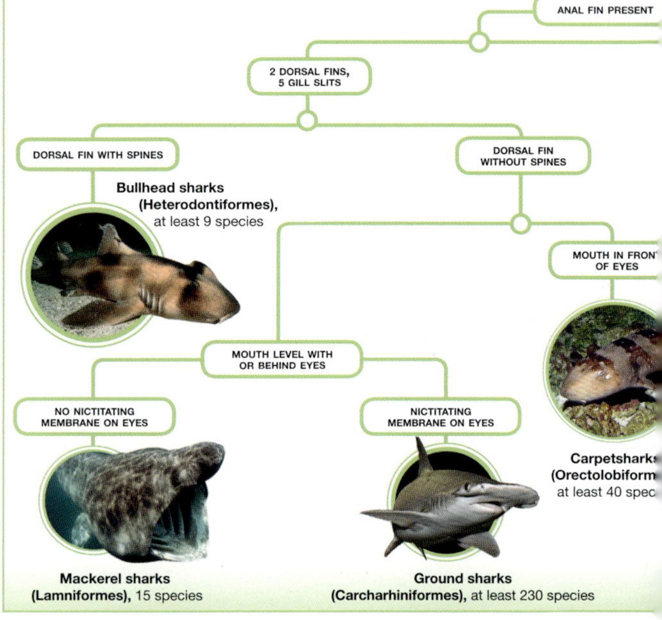

Bullhead sharks (Heterodontiformes), at least 9 species

Carpetshark (Orectolobiform at least 40 spec

Mackerel sharks (Lamniformes), 15 species

Ground sharks (Carcharhiniformes), at least 230 species

Frilled and cow sharks (Hexanchiformes), 6 species

Dogfish sharks (Squaliformes), at least 130 species

Sawsharks (Pristiophoriformes), at least 7 species

Angelsharks (Squatiniformes), at least 16 species

FOCUS ON...
FEATURES

There are a number of features that set these sharks apart from others.

▲ Sharks of this order have six or seven gills, unlike other sharks, which have just five.

▲ Hexanchiformes have only one dorsal fin, but sharks in other orders have two.

▲ The frilled shark has a uniquely shaped tail, with ribbonlike frills.

Frilled and cow sharks

With features similar to the ancient sharks such as *Cladoselache*, the frilled sharks and cow sharks are put together in the order Hexanchiformes, which has just six species.

Frilled shark

Chlamydoselachus anguineus

Named after the frilled edges to its gill slits, this weak-swimming shark is known to prey on injured or dying squid. However, it can also coil its body like a snake to launch a sudden strike, surprising its prey.

SIZE 0.97–1.17 m (3.25–3.75 ft)

HABITAT Continental shelves and slopes up to 1,000 m (3,280 ft) deep

DISTRIBUTION Western and eastern Atlantic Ocean and western, central, and eastern Pacific Ocean

Broadnose sevengill shark

Notorynchus cepedianus

The broadnose sevengill shark is easily identified as it is one of the two shark species to have seven pairs of gills. It cruises near the sea bed at a steady speed, before shooting forward to grab its prey.

SIZE 1.5–3 m (5–10 ft)

HABITAT Coastal waters and open oceans at least 136 m (446 ft) deep

DISTRIBUTION Southwestern and southeastern Atlantic Ocean, Indian Ocean, and western and eastern Pacific Ocean

Bluntnose sixgill shark

Hexanchus griseus

Also known as the cow shark, the bluntnose sixgill shark is extremely sensitive to light. During the day it swims around in the dark zone, migrating to the upper zones at night.

SIZE Up to 4.8 m (15.75 ft)

HABITAT Continental shelves and beyond up to 2,000 m (6,560 ft) deep

DISTRIBUTION Western and eastern Atlantic Ocean, Indian Ocean, and Pacific Ocean

Sharpnose sevengill shark

Heptranchias perlo

This relatively small-sized species is more active at night. It feeds on small sharks, rays, and other small fish, and in turn is hunted by larger sharks.

SIZE 85 cm (33.5 in)

HABITAT Continental shelves and slopes up to 1,000 m (3,280 ft) deep

DISTRIBUTION Atlantic Ocean, Indian Ocean, and Pacific Ocean

Dogfish sharks

The order of dogfish sharks, or Squaliformes, is made up of seven families. They are: dogfish sharks, bramble sharks, gulper sharks, sleeper sharks, lanternsharks, roughsharks, and kitefin sharks.

FOCUS ON...
FEATURES
Some dogfish sharks have unusual features.

Shortspine spurdog
Squalus mitsukurii

In some locations, this plain pearl-grey shark is known to migrate in large groups during winter months to breeding grounds for mating. It is also known as the green-eyed spurdog.

SIZE 0.7–1 m (2.3–3.3 ft)

HABITAT Continental shelves and beyond up to 954 m (3,130 ft) deep

DISTRIBUTION Atlantic Ocean, Indian Ocean, and Pacific Ocean

Piked dogfish
Squalus acanthias

While most sharks live alone or in small groups, th piked dogfish gathers in groups of thousands. Onc perhaps the most abundant shark in the world, its numbers have gradually decreased as it has bee heavily overfished for its meat. The piked dogfisl is now under threat in some localities.

SIZE 0.6–2 m (2–6.5 ft)

HABITAT Continental shelves and beyond up to 1,460 m (4,790 ft) deep

DISTRIBUTION Atlantic Ocean and Pacific Ocean

▲ The piked dogfish has a sharp spine on both
orsal fins that acts as a defence against predators.
he spines are coated with a toxic slime, which
ay be venomous to some predators.

▲ Lanternsharks have special organs that produce light. This is called bioluminescence. It may be used by the fish to attract prey in the dark, deep waters in which it lives.

An adult piked dogfish can live for more than 100 years.

Dwarf gulper shark

Centrophorus atromarginatus

The dwarf gulper shark is often confused with its larger relative, the gulper shark, because both have a grey or grey-brown body colour and widely spaced denticles. The dwarf gulper, however, can be recognized by the black markings on its fins, which the gulper shark lacks.

SIZE 60 cm (23.5 in)

HABITAT Continental shelves up to 450 m (1,480 ft) deep

DISTRIBUTION Northern and eastern Indian Ocean and western Pacific Ocean

Smallfin gulper shark

Centrophorus moluccensis

The smallfin gulper shark preys on fish and crustaceans – hard-shelled animals including crabs, shrimp, and lobsters. It has been heavily overfished in some regions for its meat.

SIZE 0.9–1.4 m (3–4.5 ft)

HABITAT Continental shelves and slopes up to 820 m (2,690 ft) deep

DISTRIBUTION Western and eastern Indian Ocean and western and southwestern Pacific Ocean

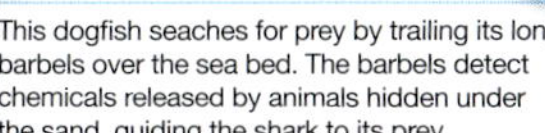

Mandarin dogfish
Cirrhigaleus barbifer

This dogfish seaches for prey by trailing its long barbels over the sea bed. The barbels detect chemicals released by animals hidden under the sand, guiding the shark to its prey.

SIZE 0.8–1.2 m (2.5–4 ft)
HABITAT Continental slopes up to 640 m (2,100 ft) deep
DISTRIBUTION Western Pacific Ocean

Longsnout dogfish
Deania quadrispinosum

The longsnout dogfish is dark brown, grey, or black. It has an extremely large snout and jaws armed with sharp cutting teeth.

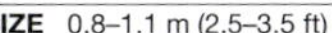

SIZE 0.8–1.1 m (2.5–3.5 ft)
HABITAT Continental shelves and slopes up to 360 m (1,180 ft) deep
DISTRIBUTION Southeastern Atlantic Ocean, western and eastern Indian Ocean, and southwestern Pacific Ocean

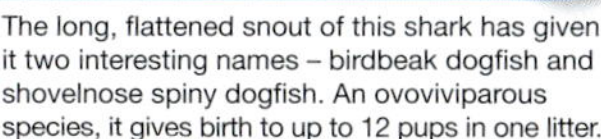

Birdbeak dogfish
Deania calcea

The long, flattened snout of this shark has given it two interesting names – birdbeak dogfish and shovelnose spiny dogfish. An ovoviviparous species, it gives birth to up to 12 pups in one litter.

SIZE 0.8–1.2 m (2.5–4 ft)
HABITAT Continental slopes up to 1,450 m (4,760 ft) deep
DISTRIBUTION Northern and eastern Atlantic Ocean, and northwestern, western, and eastern Pacific Ocean

Black dogfish
Centroscyllium fabricii

This shark has many jagged teeth with pointed ends that it uses to grab and crush the tough bodies of shellfish and small bony fish. Its dorsal fins are lined with grooved spines, which may contain mild toxins.

SIZE 0.5–1 m (1.5–3.3 ft)

HABITAT Continental shelves and beyond up to 1,600 m (5,250 ft) deep

DISTRIBUTION Western, eastern, and northern Atlantic Ocean

Blackbelly lanternshark
Etmopterus lucifer

This small shark is often found in large schools deep in the ocean. Its belly is luminescent – it emits light. The glowing bellies of these lanternsharks may enable the fish to find one another in the dark waters, keeping the schools together.

SIZE Up to 42 cm (16.5 in)

HABITAT Continental shelves and beyond up to 1,360 m (4,460 ft) deep

DISTRIBUTION Western and southwestern Pacific Ocean

Smooth lanternshark
Etmopterus pusillus

The teeth in the upper jaw of the smooth lanternshark have up to three points, while those lining the lower jaw are single-pointed and knifelike. A bottom-dwelling shark, it feeds on fish eggs, squid, and deep sea fish, such as lanternfish.

SIZE 50 cm (20 in)

HABITAT Continental slopes and beyond up to 2,000 m (6,560 ft) deep

DISTRIBUTION Western and eastern Atlantic Ocean, western Indian Ocean, and western Pacific Ocean

Velvetbelly lanternshark
Etmopterus spinax

The velvetbelly lanternshark is named after the colour of its belly, which is much darker than the rest of its body. The young of this species live in shallow waters, but as they grow older, they move to deeper waters, where there is less competition for food.

SIZE Up to 40 cm (16 in)

HABITAT Continental shelves and beyond up to 2,000 m (6,560 ft) deep

DISTRIBUTION Eastern Atlantic Ocean

Viper dogfish
Trigonognathus kabeyai

This shark feeds by using a method called ram feeding. It moves forward with its mouth open, captures the prey along with the water, and swallows it whole.

SIZE Up to 54 cm (21.25 in)

HABITAT Continental shelves and beyond up to 360 m (1,180 ft) deep

DISTRIBUTION Central and northwestern Pacific Ocean

New Zealand lanternshark
Etmopterus baxteri

The diet of a New Zealand lanternshark consists of bony fish, squid, and crustaceans such as shrimp and crabs. However, as this shark grows in size it changes its diet, feeding more on bony fish than crustaceans.

Great lanternshark
Etmopterus princeps

This ovoviviparous shark does not have dots or dashes on its sides or the pale yellow spot on top of its head like many other lanternsharks. It is thought to be a bottom-dwelling feeder, based on its diet of squid, shrimp, and crabs.

SIZE 55–75 cm (21.5–29.5 in)

HABITAT Continental slopes up to 4,500 m (14,760 ft) deep

DISTRIBUTION Northern and southeastern Atlantic Ocean

SIZE 55–88 cm (21.5–34.5 in)

HABITAT Open waters and continental shelves and slopes up to 1,400 m (4,590 ft) deep

DISTRIBUTION Southwestern Pacific Ocean and southeastern Atlantic Ocean

Caudal fin lined with hooked denticles

Slendertail lanternshark
Etmopterus molleri

This slender shark with a shiny belly is small enough to avoid being fished – so small that it can slip through the holes in nets and escape.

SIZE 46 cm (18 in)

HABITAT Continental shelves and slopes and open seas up to 860 m (2,820 ft) deep

DISTRIBUTION Western Indian Ocean and western and southwestern Pacific Ocean

Southern lanternshark
Etmopterus granulosus

The southern lanternshark has a broad head and lines of pointed denticles along its body. It has black markings on the underside of its body and tail. This shark feeds on bony fish, squid, shrimp, and crabs, and is sometimes caught by shrimp fishers.

SIZE 41 cm (16 in)

HABITAT Continental shelves and beyond up to 637 m (2,090 ft) deep

DISTRIBUTION Oceans around southern South America

Greenland shark

Somniosus microcephalus

Despite being poisonous, this shark's flesh is a delicacy in Iceland. The flesh is buried for about 12 weeks to extract the toxins.

Greenland sharks live in the freezing waters of the Arctic. They are slow swimmers and this helps them to save their energy in this environment. It is estimated that these sharks can live up to 200 years.

SIZE 3–7.3 m (10–24 ft)

HABITAT Continental shelves and slopes up to 2,200 m (7,220 ft) deep

DISTRIBUTION Arctic Ocean and northern Atlantic Ocean

Portuguese dogfish

Centroscymnus coelolepis

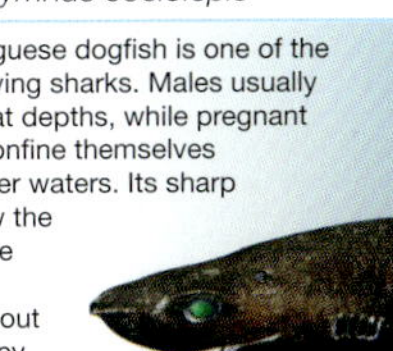

The Portuguese dogfish is one of the deepest living sharks. Males usually live at great depths, while pregnant females confine themselves to shallower waters. Its sharp teeth allow the Portuguese dogfish to take bites out of large prey.

SIZE 0.75–1 m (2.5–3.3 ft)

HABITAT Continental slopes and beyond up to 3,700 m (12,140 ft) deep

DISTRIBUTION Atlantic Ocean, Indian Ocean, and western Pacific Ocean

Longnose velvet dogfish

Centroselachus crepidater

This shark is also called the golden dogfish. Its numbers are dwindling in some areas because of overfishing as its liver oil is a source of squalene, a common ingredient in cosmetics and medicines.

SIZE 1.3 m (4.25 ft)

HABITAT Continental slopes up to 1,300 m (4,265 ft) deep

DISTRIBUTION Eastern Atlantic Ocean and parts of Indian Ocean and Pacific Ocean

Angular roughshark
Oxynotus centrina

A rare and little-known species, the angular roughshark is named for its pointed head and fins. It is sometimes used to make fishmeal and oil, or is dried and salted for human consumption.

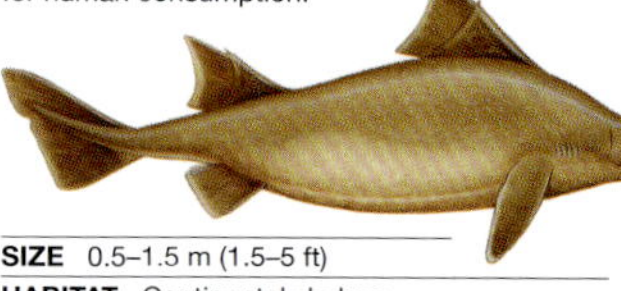

SIZE 0.5–1.5 m (1.5–5 ft)

HABITAT Continental shelves and upper slopes up to 660 m (2,165 ft) deep

DISTRIBUTION Eastern Atlantic Ocean and the Mediterranean region, except the Black Sea

Sailfin roughshark
Oxynotus paradoxus

This deepwater shark migrates upwards to the continental shelf during spring for reproduction. It eats fish and small bottom-dwelling shrimp and crabs.

SIZE Up to 1.2 m (4 ft)

HABITAT Continental slopes up to 720 m (2,360 ft) deep

DISTRIBUTION Northeastern Atlantic Ocean

Roughshark
Oxynotus bruniensis

Also known as the prickly dogfish, the skin of this shark is covered with large, prickly denticles. The roughshark has spearlike teeth in its upper jaw and bladelike teeth in its lower jaw that help it grasp and slice shrimp, crabs, and fish.

SIZE 60–90 cm (23.5–35 in)

HABITAT Outer continental shelves and beyond up to 1,070 m (3,510 ft) deep

DISTRIBUTION Southwestern Pacific Ocean

A weak swimmer, the roughshark relies on its large, oily liver to float above the sea bed.

Kitefin shark
Dalatias licha

A solitary hunter, the kitefin shark preys on crabs, fish, rays, and other sharks. The large, knifelike teeth on its lower jaw form a continuous cutting edge, allowing it to take bites out of prey bigger than itself.

SIZE 0.8–1.6 m (2.5–5.25 ft)

HABITAT Outer continental shelves and beyond up to 1,800 m (5,905 ft) deep

DISTRIBUTION Eastern and western Atlantic Ocean, central and western Pacific Ocean, and western Indian Ocean

Cookiecutter shark
Isistius brasiliensis

The cookiecutter shark has a circular mouth with strong jaws and sawlike lower teeth, which can take circular cookie-shaped bites out of its prey. It has light-emitting organs on the underside of its body, which attract large predators to investigate. The cookiecutter then becomes the hunter, taking a bite out of the would-be predator.

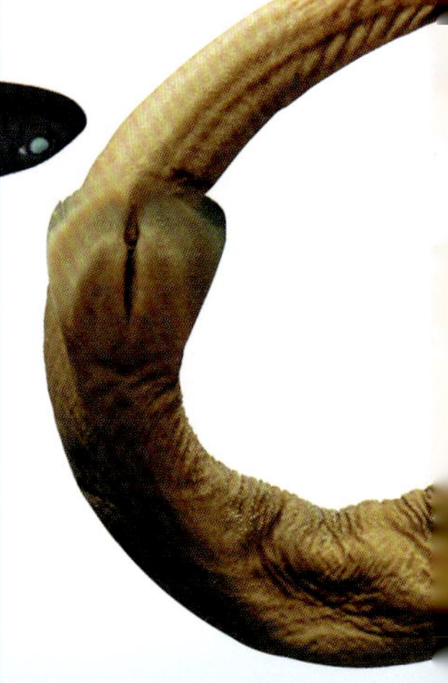

SIZE Up to 56 cm (22 in)

HABITAT Around oceanic islands and open oceans up to 3,500 m (11,480 ft) deep

DISTRIBUTION Atlantic Ocean, Pacific Ocean, and Indian Ocean

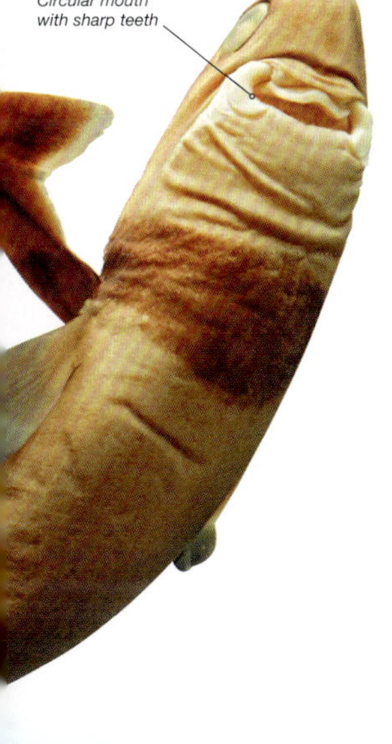

Circular mouth with sharp teeth

Pygmy shark

Euprotomicrus bispinatus

The pygmy shark is one of the smallest sharks in the world. During the day, it swims in the dark zone to feed on squid, bony fish, and crustaceans, and at night, it swims to the water surface.

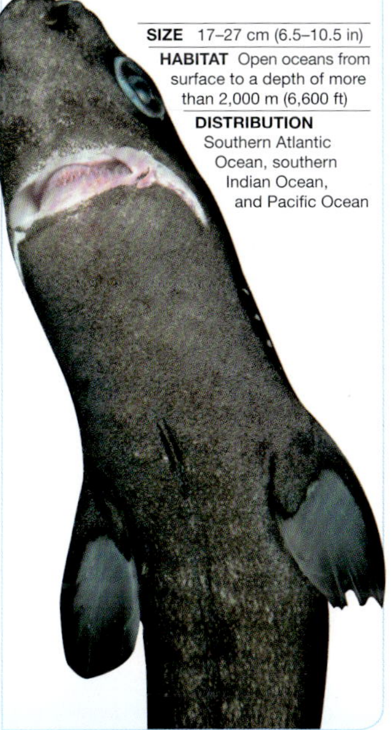

SIZE 17–27 cm (6.5–10.5 in)

HABITAT Open oceans from surface to a depth of more than 2,000 m (6,600 ft)

DISTRIBUTION Southern Atlantic Ocean, southern Indian Ocean, and Pacific Ocean

Sawsharks

The order of sawsharks, or Pristiophoriformes, contains at least seven species. The most distinctive feature of these sharks is the long, sawlike snout edged with teeth of varied length. They look similar to sawfish, a kind of ray, but sawfish teeth are more even.

Japanese sawshark

Pristiophorus japonicus

Like most sawsharks, this shark can search for prey by trailing its barbels across the sea bed and using its snout to dig out hidden crabs and other crustaceans. It is found near the coasts of Japan, Korea, and China.

SIZE 0.8–1.5 m (2.5–5 ft)

HABITAT Continental shelves and beyond up to 800 m (2,625 ft) deep

DISTRIBUTION Northwestern Pacific Ocean

Tropical sawshark

Pristiophorus delicatus

This rare shark was only described as a separate species in 2008 and little is known about it. Tropical sawsharks live only in a small region off the coast of Queensland, Australia.

SIZE Up to 85 cm (33.5 in)

HABITAT Outer continental shelves and upper slopes up to 405 m (1,330 ft) deep

DISTRIBUTION Northeastern Australia

FOCUS ON... SNOUT

A sawshark's snout is a useful, if deadly, weapon.

▲ Sawsharks use the length of their snout to attack prey and defend against predators. The sharp teeth act as blades, cutting through flesh and inflicting a crippling wound.

Longnose sawshark

Pristiophorus cirratus

This ovoviviparous shark gives birth to 3–22 pups per litter. The teeth of the newborn pups are folded against their snout, which protects the mother from harm. The longnose sawshark eats small bony fish, and sometimes crustaceans such as crabs and shrimp.

SIZE Up to 1.5 m (5 ft)

HABITAT Continental shelves and beyond up to 310 m (1,020 ft) deep

DISTRIBUTION Eastern Indian Ocean and Pacific Ocean

Barbel on snout

FOCUS ON...
FEATURES
Angelsharks have unusual adaptations to help their hide-and-strike hunting method.

▲ The flattened body and camouflaged skin of an angelshark allows it to hide, unmoving, on the sea bed.

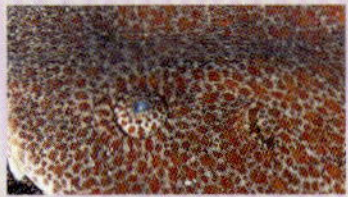

▲ Angelsharks leave their spiracles exposed in order to breathe as they lie under the sand.

▲ Unlike other sharks, they can flatten their dorsal fins and tail fin on to the sea bed.

Angelsharks

The 16 species that make up the order Squatiniformes, or angelsharks, are very different in appearance from other sharks. They have flattened bodies and broad pectoral fins, which allow them to hide under sand in order to ambush prey.

Common angelshark

ENDANGERED

Squatina squatina

The common angelshark is found on sandy or rocky bottoms, or in seagrass beds, where it lies hidden under sand, waiting for prey. It feeds mainly on flatfish, skates, crustaceans, and molluscs.

SIZE 0.8–2.4 m (2.5–8 ft)

HABITAT Continental shelves up to 150 m (492 ft) deep

DISTRIBUTION Northern Atlantic Ocean, Mediterranean Sea, and Black Sea

Japanese angelshark

Squatina japonica

The front half of this species looks like a ray, but the rear looks like a shark. Like other angelsharks, it can extend its "neck" to gulp down prey that swim overhead.

SIZE Up to 2 m (6.5 ft)

HABITAT Continental shelves up to 300 m (984 ft) deep

DISTRIBUTION Northwestern Pacific Ocean

Australian angelshark

Squatina australis

The Australian angelshark is an ovoviviparous species that can give birth to up to 20 pups per litter. Its blunt snout and nostrils have fringed skin flaps that probably help detect prey by touch, taste, or smell.

SIZE Up to 1.5 m (5 ft)

HABITAT Continental shelves and beyond up to 255 m (840 ft) deep

DISTRIBUTION Southeastern Indian Ocean and southwestern Pacific Ocean

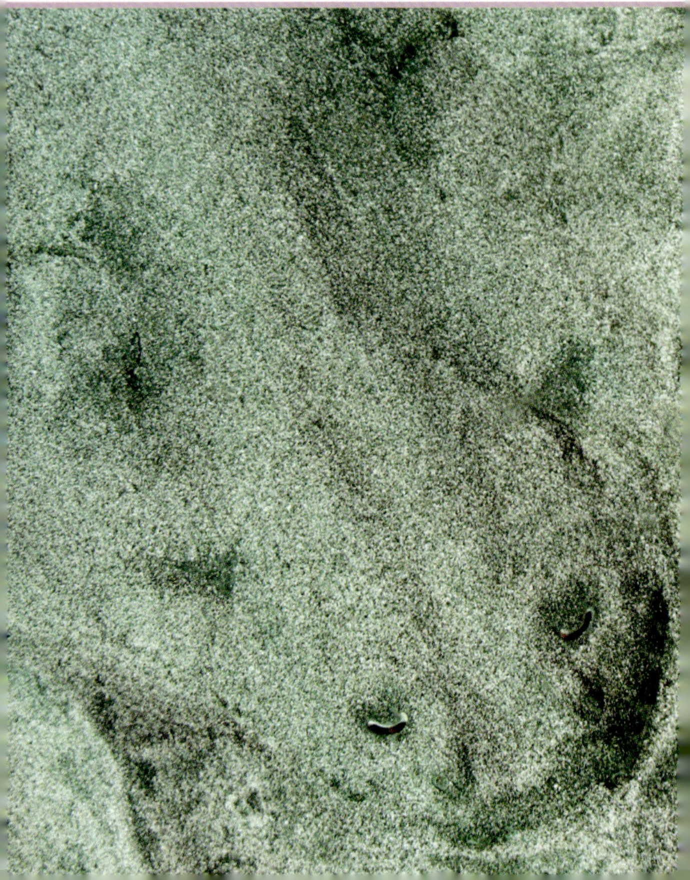

Hiding in the sand with barely its eyes exposed, the angelshark becomes almost invisible

ANGELSHARK

Angelsharks are benthic sharks, which means they live on the sea bed. They are ambush predators, hiding in the sand to launch a surprise attack on prey. These sharks get their name because their pectoral and pelvic fins spread wide, like the wings of an angel.

Pacific angelshark

Squatina californica

It takes just one-tenth of a second for this shark to rise up from under the sand and snap up a passing fish in its jaws.

Commonly found in flat sands and reefs, this shark is recognized by the cone-shaped barbels on its snout. At night, the Pacific angelshark uses the light emitted by certain plankton to find its prey. When a fish passes through the swarm, the plankton give out light, which gives away its location to the hungry angelshark.

SIZE 1–1.5 m (3.3–5 ft)

HABITAT Continental shelves up to 200 m (656 ft) deep

DISTRIBUTION Northeastern and southeastern Pacific Ocean

Barbel on snout

Sand devil

Squatina dumeril

Also known as the Atlantic angelshark, the sand devil is often mistaken for a ray because of its flat body and winglike fins. This fish is ovoviviparous, with up to 25 pups being born in each litter.

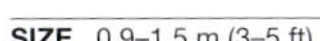

SIZE 0.9–1.5 m (3–5 ft)

HABITAT Continental shelves and beyond up to 250 m (820 ft) deep

DISTRIBUTION Northwestern Atlantic Ocean and Gulf of Mexico

Ornate angelshark

Squatina tergocellata

The ornate angelshark preys mainly on fish and squid, some of which have poisonous flesh. In order to keep the poison from affecting it, the angelshark swallows mud that acts as a buffer against the poison.

SIZE Up to 1.4 m (4.5 ft)

HABITAT Continental shelves and beyond up to 400 m (1,310 ft) deep

DISTRIBUTION Southeastern Indian Ocean

Bullhead sharks

The nine species of bullhead sharks form the order Heterodontiformes. These little blunt-headed sharks mostly feed on crustaceans, such as crabs and shrimp.

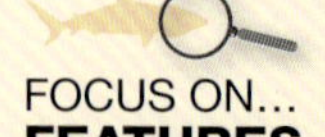

FOCUS ON...
FEATURES
Bullhead sharks have combination of featur that sets them apart.

Mexican hornshark
Heterodontus mexicanus

This slender-bodied shark is fished by humans for its meat and skin. The eggs of this oviparous species have long tendrils that help anchor the eggs to rocks and seaweed.

SIZE 40–50 cm (16–20 in)

HABITAT Continental shelves up to 50 m (164 ft) deep

DISTRIBUTION Eastern Pacific Ocean

Port Jackson shark
Heterodontus portusjacksoni

This shark has dark brown markings on a light grey-brown body. It is most active at night, when it feeds. It is not fished because its flesh and fins are considered to be of poor quality.

SIZE 75 cm (29.5 in)

HABITAT Coastal reefs up to 245 m (805 ft) dee

DISTRIBUTION Eastern Indian Ocean and southwestern Pacific Ocean

▲ These sharks have a mall spine on the front of each of their two dorsal fins.

▲ They have flat teeth at the back of their jaws for crushing the hard shells of their prey.

▲ The eggs of these sharks are spiral-shaped, which allows them to become wedged in cracks, protecting them from predators.

Horn shark

Heterodontus francisci

The horn shark can survive more than 12 years, in captivity – in aquariums to educate and entertain people, and where endangered sharks can be raised to preserve the species. This slow-moving predator prefers to hunt at night and take shelter during the day.

SIZE 56–61 cm (22–24 in)

HABITAT Continental shelves at least 150 m (500 ft) deep

DISTRIBUTION Eastern Pacific Ocean

The fin spines of the horn shark are used in making jewellery.

Zebra bullhead shark
Heterodontus zebra

This shark is named for its pattern of zebra-like black stripes. It preys on other sharks' eggcases, biting through their hard covering with its teeth.

SIZE 0.6–1.2 m (2–4 ft)

HABITAT Continental shelves up to 220 m (720 ft) deep

DISTRIBUTION Western Pacific Ocean and eastern Indian Ocean

Japanese bullhead shark
Heterodontus japonicus

This popular Japanese aquarium pet can use its pectoral and pelvic fins to "walk" along the sea bed while searching for food.

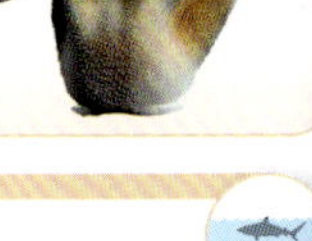

SIZE 0.7–1.2 m (2.3–4 ft)

HABITAT Continental shelves up to 37 m (120 ft) deep

DISTRIBUTION Northwestern Pacific Ocean

Galápagos bullhead shark
Heterodontus quoyi

A nocturnal predator, the Galápagos bullhead shark can often be seen resting on underwater ledges during the day. At night, it forages the sea bed for prey, including shellfish, crabs, and molluscs.

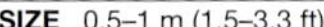

SIZE 0.5–1 m (1.5–3.3 ft)

HABITAT Coral reefs up to 30 m (98 ft) deep

DISTRIBUTION Eastern Pacific Ocean

Crested bullhead shark
Heterodontus galeatus

This rare bullhead shark can be recognized by the large ridges above its eyes and dark blotches on its body. The crested bullhead shark eats the eggcases of the Port Jackson shark.

SIZE 60 cm (23.5 in)

HABITAT Continental shelves up to 93 m (305 ft) deep

DISTRIBUTION Western Pacific Ocean

The crested bullhead shark holds a tough eggcase with its front teeth and crushes it with those at the back to suck out the contents.

FOCUS ON...
PATTERNS
This order gets its name from the skin patterns in many of the sharks.

▲ Zebra sharks have a dotted, brown-on-white pattern across their body.

▲ Each whale shark has a unique pattern of spots and stripes.

▲ A wobbegong's pattern breaks up its outline, helping it to hide in reefs.

Carpetsharks

The order of carpetsharks, or Orectolobiformes, has more than 30 species. Sharks of this diverse group range in size from the barbelthroat (33 cm/13 in long) to the whale shark (18 m/59 ft) – the world's largest fish.

Collared carpetshark

Parascyllium collare

This shark gets its name from the dark chocolate brown or black collar that grows over its gills. The lack of white spots on its collar makes it look different from the necklace carpetshark.

SIZE Up to 87 cm (34.25 in)

HABITAT Continental shelves up to 160 m (525 ft) deep

DISTRIBUTION
Southwestern Pacific Ocean

Necklace carpetshark
Parascyllium variolatum

This small shark's bold, beautiful colour pattern includes a speckled "necklace". It feeds mainly on bony fish, crabs, lobsters, crayfish, shrimp, krill, and molluscs.

SIZE Up to 90 cm (35 in)

HABITAT Continental shelves up to 180 m (590 ft) deep

DISTRIBUTION
Eastern Indian Ocean and southwestern Pacific Ocean

Bluegrey carpetshark
Heteroscyllium colcloughi

Also known as Colclough's shark, the bluegrey carpetshark is a rare species found only on the eastern coast of Australia. The young have black-and-white colour patterns that fade with age.

SIZE 50–75 cm (20–29.5 in)

HABITAT Continental shelves in inshore waters

DISTRIBUTION Western Pacific Ocean

Blind shark
Brachaelurus waddi

This small, stout shark gets its name from its habit of shutting its eyes when removed from water. The blind shark is known to have survived for up to 18 hours out of water.

SIZE 60–70 cm (23.5–28 in)

HABITAT Coral reefs up to at least 110 m (360 ft) deep

DISTRIBUTION
Western Pacific Ocean

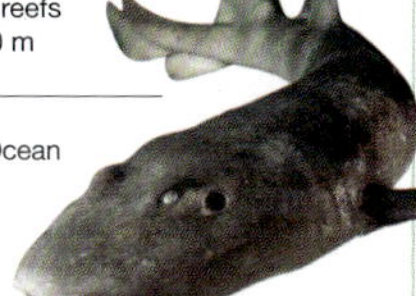

Whale shark
Rhincodon typus

Tawny nurse shark
Nebrius ferrugineus

During the day, the tawny nurse shark can be found resting in gatherings of 20 or more sharks inside caves or on ledges. Hunting at night, the shark uses its strong jaws to suck out prey hiding inside holes and crevices.

SIZE Up to 3.2 m (10.5 ft)

HABITAT Rocky or sandy sea beds up to 70 m (230 ft) deep

DISTRIBUTION Indo-Pacific (Red Sea and waters off East Africa to French Polynesian Islands)

Zebra shark
Stegostoma fasciatum

Zebra shark pups are patterned like zebras, with yellow stripes on a brown body. As they grow up, the pattern breaks up into brown spots on yellow.

The broad tail fin can be as long as rest of the body

The whale shark is the world's biggest fish. However, it is one of only three shark species to feed on tiny prey. It has a large mouth and eats plants and animals by filtering them through its comblike gill rakers.

SIZE 6–18 m (20–59 ft)

HABITAT Open oceans up to 700 m (2,300 ft) deep

DISTRIBUTION All tropical and warm temperate seas, except the Mediterranean Sea

Broad, flat head with a short snout

SIZE Up to 3.5 m (11.5 ft)

HABITAT Coral reefs and rocky and sandy sea beds up to 65 m (210 ft) deep

DISTRIBUTION Indian Ocean and western Pacific Ocean

Nurse shark

Ginglymostoma cirratum

A nocturnal hunter, this shark spends the day resting in large groups on sand or in caves. After hunting, it returns to the same resting place every day. It has a small mouth but a large throat cavity to suck in its prey.

SIZE Up to 3 m (10 ft)

HABITAT Coastal reefs and sandy sea beds up to 130 m (427 ft) deep

DISTRIBUTION Western and eastern Atlantic Ocean and eastern Pacific Ocean

whale shark's mouth can row to 1.5 m (5 ft) wide nd contain more than 300 rows f tiny teeth, each no bigger an a match head

WHALE SHARK

The gill rakers in the throat of a whale shark help it to filter plankton, krill, small fish, and squid from the water. However, it is not unusual for fish to swim alongside the shark – its large size deters other predators from pursuing them.

Japanese wobbegong

Orectolobus japonicus

This small, boldly patterned wobbegong is nocturnal. The Japanese wobbegong hunts for shrimp, squid, octopuses and small fish. It eats shark eggcases too.

SIZE Up to 1 m (3.3 ft)

HABITAT Coral reefs and rocky sea beds up to 200 m (656 ft) deep

DISTRIBUTION Northwestern Pacific Ocean

Ornate wobbegong

Orectolobus ornatus

The ornate wobbegong shark uses its fanglike teeth to capture its prey, which include bony fish, sharks, and rays. The shark rests in groups by day and hunts at night.

SIZE 0.6–1.8 m (2–6 ft)

HABITAT Coral reefs and rocky sea beds up to 100 m (328 ft) deep

DISTRIBUTION Southeastern Indian Ocean and southwestern Pacific Ocean

Tasselled wobbegong

Eucrossorhinus dasypogon

This mainly nocturnal shark lives within a fixed range on the coral reefs. A solitary animal, the shark rests during the day inside caves and ledges, often eating the small fish that share its resting place.

SIZE Up to 1.3 m (4.25 ft)

HABITAT Coral reefs up to 40 m (131 ft) deep

DISTRIBUTION Eastern Indian Ocean and western Pacific Ocean

Cobbler wobbegong

Sutorectus tentaculatus

Irregular spots, colourful patterns, and wartlike growths give the cobbler wobbegong's body an irregular outline. This allows the shark to camouflage itself on the reefs, making it a very efficient ambush predator.

SIZE 70–90 cm (28–35 in)

HABITAT Coral reefs

DISTRIBUTION Southeastern Indian Ocean

An ornate wobbegong can hold large prey in its mouth for days, impaled on its

fanglike teeth

ORNATE WOBBEGONG
The ornate wobbegong is perfectly camouflaged among coral reefs and seaweed while it lies in wait to ambush its prey. It can use its fleshy barbels as lures to attract prey, which is quickly snapped up in its jaws.

Brownbanded bambooshark
Chiloscyllium punctatum

The brownbanded bambooshark is a popular aquarium shark as it needs little space to swim. In the wild it can survive for hours out of water when stranded by the outgoing tide.

SIZE Up to 1.2 m (4 ft)

HABITAT Coral reefs and nearby sandy sea beds

DISTRIBUTION Northeastern and eastern Indian Ocean and western Pacific Ocean

White-spotted bambooshark
Chiloscyllium plagiosum

A common, yet little-known species, the white-spotted bambooshark is mainly caught for its flesh and for use in Chinese medicines. It feeds on crustaceans and bony fish.

SIZE Up to 95 cm (37.5 in)

HABITAT Coral reefs and nearby sandy sea beds

DISTRIBUTION Indian Ocean and western Pacific Ocean

Epaulette carpetshark
Hemiscyllium ocellatum

This shark uses its two front paddlelike fins to "walk" among the reefs, feeding on fish, worms, and crabs. On each side of its body, the shark has a large black spot ringed with white, which looks like an epaulette (soldiers' shoulder decoration).

SIZE Up to 1.07 m (3.5 ft)

HABITAT Coral reefs up to 50 m (164 ft) deep

DISTRIBUTION Eastern Indian Ocean and southwestern Pacific Ocean

Papuan epaulette carpetshark
Hemiscyllium hallstromi

The slender, eel-like body of the Papuan epaulette carpetshark allows it to move easily through confined spaces when searching for prey. It uses its muscular fins to wriggle or clamber over the sea bed.

SIZE Up to 75 cm (29.5 in)

HABITAT Coral reefs

DISTRIBUTION
Western central Pacific Ocean

Milne Bay epaulette shark

Hemiscyllium michaeli

Until 2010, this epaulette shark was considered to be the same species as the Indonesian speckled carpetshark. This shark can be told apart from the Indonesian speckled carpetshark by the leopardlike brown spots on its back, as well as the well-defined black spot behind its head.

SIZE Up to 69.5 cm (27 in)

HABITAT Coral reefs and shallow sandy sea beds

DISTRIBUTION Western Pacific Ocean (Eastern Papua New Guinea)

Arabian carpetshark

Chiloscyllium arabicum

The Arabian carpetshark has a long, slender, and almost cylindrical body with a long tail. It moves over coral reefs in search of prey, using its barbels to sense chemicals in the water.

SIZE 50–70 cm (20–28 in)

HABITAT Coral reefs and sandy or rocky sea beds up to 100 m (328 ft) deep

DISTRIBUTION Northern Indian Ocean and Persian Gulf

Barbel is used for sensing prey

Hooded carpetshark

Hemiscyllium strahani

The head of this shark is paler than its body, giving it the appearance of wearing a hood. This species is under threat due to habitat destruction and capture for use as an aquarium fish.

SIZE 50–80 cm (20–32 in)

HABITAT Coral reefs up to 18 m (59 ft) deep

DISTRIBUTION Western Pacific Ocean (Eastern Papua New Guinea)

Mackerel sharks

The order of mackerel sharks, or Lamniformes, has existed for more than 120 million years. It includes some of the fastest sharks in the world, such as the great white and the shortfin mako.

FOCUS ON...
TEETH
The various species of this group have differer type of teeth dependin on their prey.

Sandtiger shark
Carcharias taurus

The sandtiger shark gulps air at the surface of the sea and stores it in its stomach. This allows it to stay almost motionless without having to swim. Using this technique, the shark can drift quietly towards its prey before attacking it.

SIZE 2.5–3.2 m (8.25–10.5 ft)

HABITAT Continental shelves up to 190 m (625 ft) deep

DISTRIBUTION Warm oceans worldwide, except central and eastern Pacific Ocean

Goblin shark
Mitsukurina owstoni

The deep-living goblin shark can extend its jaws to reach out to prey. With a sucking motion, it draws the prey into its mouth and impales it on its teeth.

SIZE 2.6–6.2 m (8.5–20.3 ft)

HABITAT Continental shelves and slopes at least 980 m (3,210 ft) deep

DISTRIBUTION Pacific Ocean, Atlantic Ocean, and Indian Ocean

Basking sharks have tiny
ɪth, but they do not eat with
ɪm. They feed by straining food
ɪm the water with their gills.

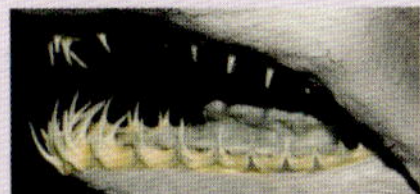

▲ The goblin shark has sharp teeth at the front of its mouth, which are used for stabbing squid, crabs, and fish.

▲ The teeth of the great white are triangular in shape, with serrated edges that help to tear off chunks of meat from its prey.

ꞩmalltooth sandtiger shark

)dontaspis ferox

ɪis warm-water shark is known to return
ɔ the same location year after year in search
f prey, which include bony fish, squid, and
ɾabs. Its body colour varies according
ɔ the region in which it is found.

ɪIZE 2–4.5 m (6.5–14.75 ft)

ɪABITAT Continental shelves
p to at least 180 m (590 ft) deep

ɪISTRIBUTION Atlantic Ocean, Indian
ɔcean, and Pacific Ocean

This shark has a large oily liver, which allows it to stay afloat with little effort.

Crocodile shark
Pseudocarcharias kamoharai

This deepwater shark has large eyes for seeing in dim light. It extends its jaws to grab small fish and other prey with its stabbing teeth.

SIZE 0.7–1.1 m (2.3–3.5 ft)

HABITAT Open oceans up to 590 m (1,935 ft) deep

DISTRIBUTION Tropical waters of the Atlantic Ocean, Indian Ocean, and Pacific Ocean

Megamouth shark
Megachasma pelagios

The megamouth shark hunts its prey in deep water during the day but moves upwards at night, following its prey. This shark sucks in water through its mouth, filtering out animal plankton with its gill rakers.

SIZE 5.5–7.1 m (18–23.3 ft)

HABITAT Inshore, offshore, and oceanic waters up to 1,000 m (3,280 ft) deep

DISTRIBUTION Warm waters of the Atlantic Ocean, Indian Ocean, and Pacific Ocean

Basking shark
Cetorhinus maximus

Basking sharks are the second-largest fish in the ocean after whale sharks. They are filter feeders and in summer can be seen near the surface, swimming with their mouths wide open taking in water laden with krill and other plankto

A basking shark's liver makes up a quarter of its entire body weight.

SIZE 7–12.3 m (23–40.4 ft)

HABITAT Inshore and offshore waters up to 1,265 m (4,150 ft) deep

DISTRIBUTION Temperate waters of the Atlantic Ocean, Pacific Ocean, and parts of the Indian Ocean

Female basking sharks may have pregnancies that last for three years

BASKING SHARK
The basking shark gets its name from its habit of swimming slowly in sunlit waters near the ocean's surface. However, it can also dive to depths of 900 m (2,950 ft) to feed on plankton.

Thresher shark
Alopias vulpinus

This shark uses its long tail fin to round up shoals of fish and even stun them before killing them. Sometimes they attack in pairs. A very strong swimmer, the thresher shark is one of the few shark species known to jump fully out of water.

SIZE 2.7–6 m (9–20 ft)

HABITAT Continental shelves and beyond up to at least 365 m (1,200 ft) deep

DISTRIBUTION Atlantic Ocean, Indian Ocean, and Pacific Ocean

Pelagic thresher shark
Alopias pelagicus

The pelagic thresher shark is the smallest of the thresher species. It is often confused with the thresher shark as it is similar in appearance. The upper lobe of the tail fin is often as long as the shark's body. This ocean-living shark is known to swim to shallow waters in the morning where it allows certain species of fish to eat the dead skin and parasites on its body. This provides the shark with a cleaning service, while the fish get a meal.

SIZE 2.5–3 m (8.25–10 ft)

HABITAT Open oceans up to 150 m (500 ft) deep

DISTRIBUTION Indian Ocean and southern Pacific Ocean

Bigeye thresher shark

Alopias superciliosus

The large eyes of the bigeye thresher shark are adapted for hunting in low light. It hunts by looking for silhouettes of its prey in the dim light. This shark stays in deep water during the day and moves upwards to feed in surface waters at night.

SIZE 3–4.6 m (10–15 ft)

HABITAT Continental shelves and beyond up to at least 720 m (2,370 ft) deep

DISTRIBUTION Atlantic Ocean, Indian Ocean, and Pacific Ocean

A newborn pup of a pelagic thresher shark can be half as long as its mother.

Salmon shark
Lamna ditropis

As its name suggests, this shark feeds mainly on salmon. Like the great white, short fin mako, and porbeagle sharks, it can maintain a high body temperature, allowing it to hunt actively in cool water.

SIZE 1.8–3 m (6–10 ft)

HABITAT Cool coastal or oceanic waters up to 250 m (820 ft) deep

DISTRIBUTION Northern Pacific Ocean

Porbeagle shark
Lamna nasus

Porbeagle sharks can migrate long distances of 2,000 km (1,240 miles) or more, travelling between feeding areas and breeding areas.

SIZE 1.5–3 m (5–10 ft)

HABITAT Inshore to offshore waters up to 370 m (1,215 ft) deep

DISTRIBUTION Southern Atlantic Ocean, southern Indian Ocean, southern Pacific Ocean, and Southern Ocean

Great white shark
Carcharodon carcharias

One of the world's largest predators, the great white shark is not always easily noticed by its prey because of its colouring. When prey looks up from below, the shark's white belly looks like a patch of sunlight. When seen from the side, the light reflects differently off the belly compared to the grey back, breaking up the shark's outline. This is known as countershading.

SIZE 3.5–6.4 m (11.5–21 ft)

HABITAT Coastal, inshore, and offshore waters up to 1,220 m (4,000 ft) deep

DISTRIBUTION Cool to warm waters of the Atlantic Ocean, Indian Ocean, and Pacific Ocean

Most great white attacks on people stem from curiosity or mistaken identity.

Shortfin mako

Isurus oxyrinchus

This shark attacks its prey at a great speed from below, swimming beneath its prey and then rushing upwards to attack and tear off flesh. It is thought to reach speeds of 75 kph (46.5 mph).

SIZE 2–3.9 m (6.5–13 ft)

HABITAT Coastal waters and open oceans up to 500 m (1,640 ft) deep

DISTRIBUTION Warm to temperate waters of the Atlantic Ocean, Indian Ocean, and Pacific Ocean

GREAT WHITE SHARK
The great white shark is one of the most efficient predators in the world. Like many other sharks, its ampullae of Lorenzini can detect the weak electrical signals of its prey when close. It can probably sense electric fields that are a million times weaker than humans can sense.

A great white shark can sniff out a single drop of

blood

in 100 litres (26.4 gal) of water

Ground sharks

With more than 230 species, ground sharks, or Carcharhiniformes, form the largest order. It is made up of eight families, including catsharks and hammerheads.

FOCUS ON...
HABITATS
The different species in this order live in varied habitats across the world.

Longnose catshark
Apristurus kampae

Newborn pups have two rows of enlarged denticles on their back that help them break out of the egg case. These disappear soon after birth.

This is an oviparous species that feeds on shrimp, squid, and small fish. Since it lives in deep waters, the longnose catshark is rarely caught and so very little is known about it.

SIZE Up to 52 cm (20.5 in)

HABITAT Continental slopes up to 1,900 m (6,235 ft) deep

DISTRIBUTION Northeastern and southeastern Pacific Ocean

▲ The roughskin catshark is found in deep waters beyond the continental shelves.

▲ The coral catshark prefers to spend its time in holes and caves in coral reefs.

▲ The grey reef shark can be found hunting for prey over reefs and near coasts.

Deepwater catshark

Apristurus profundorum

The deepwater catshark is a small, sluggish fish with a thick, flattened snout. Its skin has a feltlike texture, which gives it a fuzzy appearance. It has rather prominent gill slits and a long tail fin. It feeds on crustaceans, squid, and small fish.

SIZE At least 50 cm (20 in)

HABITAT Continental slopes up to 1,750 m (5,740 ft) deep

DISTRIBUTION Western and eastern Atlantic Ocean

Roughskin catshark

Apristurus ampliceps

The roughskin catshark has a brown or black-brown body. Like other deepwater sharks, it often escapes being caught, as it lives in a deep zone where fishing nets rarely, if ever, reach.

SIZE 67–86 cm (26.3–34 in)

HABITAT Continental slopes up to 1,500 m (4,920 ft) deep

DISTRIBUTION Southwestern Pacific Ocean

Grey spotted catshark
Asymbolus analis

This little-researched catshark is found near southeastern Australia. It is caught as bycatch by trawler fishermen, and may be vulnerable to unintended overfishing.

SIZE 45–60 cm (18–23.5 in)

HABITAT Continental shelves up to 175 m (575 ft) deep

DISTRIBUTION Western Pacific Ocean

Western spotted catshark
Asymbolus occiduus

This catshark is found only around southwestern Australia. Like other small catsharks, it can only be trapped by nets with small meshes. Being quite numerous, it is less vulnerable than the grey spotted catshark to accidental overfishing.

Orange spotted catshark
Asymbolus rubiginosus

Often caught as bycatch, this oviparous catshark's numbers are less affected by trawling because of its continuous egg-laying cycle. The next batch of eggs are laid before, as soon as, or just after the previous pups hatch. This helps maintain its numbers.

SIZE 35–55 cm (14–21.5 in)

HABITAT Continental shelves and beyond up to 540 m (1,770 ft) deep

DISTRIBUTION Western Pacific Ocean

SIZE 58–60 cm (23–23.5 in)

HABITAT Outer continental shelves up to 98–250 m (322–820 ft) deep

DISTRIBUTION Eastern Indian Ocean

The number of females carrying eggs is highest in spring, intermediate in autumn, and lowest in winter.

Coral catshark

Atelomycterus marmoratus

The coral catshark hides in reefs and remains inactive during the day, coming out at dusk and at night to hunt for squid and small bony fish. This small shark is harmless and attractive, and so is a popular choice for aquariums.

SIZE 40–70 cm (16–28 in)

HABITAT Coral reefs

DISTRIBUTION Western Pacific Ocean

Blackmouth catshark

Galeus melastomus

The blackmouth catshark spends its time near the muddy sea bed. It relies heavily on its ampullae of Lorenzini to hunt prey in these dark waters. Young sharks tend to swim in shallower waters than the adults.

SIZE 35–80 cm (14–32 in)

HABITAT Continental shelves and beyond up to 1,000 m (3,280 ft) deep

DISTRIBUTION Northeastern Atlantic Ocean and Mediterranean Sea

Draughtsboard catshark
Cephaloscyllium isabellum

The draughtsboard catshark defends itself against predators by hiding inside holes among rocks or reefs and sucking in water. This inflates its body and wedges it inside the hole, making it difficult for a predator to pull it out.

SIZE 0.6–1.5 m (2–5 ft)

HABITAT Sandy and rocky sea beds up to 670 m (2,210 ft) deep

DISTRIBUTION Coastal and offshore waters around New Zealand

Swell shark
Cephaloscyllium ventriosum

Like the draughtsboard catshark, this shark swallows water to prevent predators from pulling it out of its hiding place. During an attack, it may also hold its tail in its mouth to stop other fish from getting hold of it.

SIZE 0.8–1 m (2.5–3.3 ft)

HABITAT Continental shelves up to 460 m (1,510 ft) deep

DISTRIBUTION Eastern Pacific Ocean

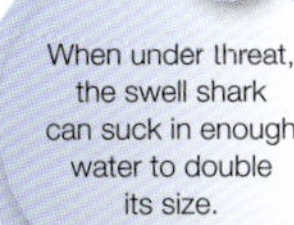

When under threat, the swell shark can suck in enough water to double its size.

Striped catshark
Poroderma africanum

This shark is also known as the pyjama shark because of the dark stripes on its body that run from nose to tail. These stripes help it to blend in with the surrounding rocks and reefs.

SIZE 60–95 cm (23.5–37.5 in)

HABITAT Coastal and offshore areas up to 280 m (920 ft) deep

DISTRIBUTION Southeastern Atlantic Ocean and southwestern Indian Ocean

Leopard catshark
Poroderma pantherinum

Dark shyshark
Haploblepharus pictus

The dark shyshark gets its name from its habit of curling into a ring with its tail covering its eyes when threatened. Until recently, the dark shyshark was regarded by some to be the same species as the puffadder shyshark.

‑he markings on this shark depend on its age and ‑ocation. Newborn pups have black spots, but as ‑hey grow, these spots can become smaller, and ‑sometimes merge into lines. Densely spotted sharks ‑re found off the Eastern Cape of South Africa.

SIZE Up to 84 cm (33 in)

HABITAT Rocky sea beds up to 250 m (820 ft) deep

DISTRIBUTION Southwestern Indian Ocean and southeastern Atlantic Ocean

‑IZE Up to 60 cm (23.5 in)

‑ABITAT Rocky sea beds up to 35 m ‑15 ft) deep

‑ISTRIBUTION Southeastern Atlantic Ocean ‑nd western Indian Ocean around South Africa

Puffadder shyshark

Haploblepharus edwardsii

This shark is also known as "happy Eddie". This species is more slender than other shysharks. It is sluggish and reclusive and is often seen lying still on the sea bed.

SIZE Up to 69 cm (27 in)

HABITAT Sandy or rocky sea beds up to 130 m (427 ft) deep

DISTRIBUTION Southeastern Atlantic Ocean and southwestern Indian Ocean

Chain catshark
Scyliorhinus retifer

Also known as the chain dogfish, the chain catshark is an oviparous species, and lays eggs in pairs. Each egg has two coiled tendrils that can attach to rocky surfaces, keeping the egg from being washed away. A sluggish species, it leaves the sea bed only occasionally, with adults preferring rocky surfaces. This catshark feeds on squid, bony fish, and crustaceans.

SIZE Up to 59 cm (23.25 in)

HABITAT Continental shelves and beyond to at least 754 m (2,475 ft) deep

DISTRIBUTION Northwestern and western central Atlantic Ocean, Gulf of Mexico, and Caribbean Sea

The skin of the chain catshark glows in the dark, but no one has yet been able to discover why.

·mallspotted catshark

·cyliorhinus canicula

This shark's skin has a sandpaper-like texture

·ne smallspotted catshark, also known as the ·sser spotted dogfish, is known to use its ·enticles when feeding. After grasping prey in · jaws, the shark curls its tail towards its mouth, ·ooking its denticles into the prey. It then flicks its ·ead back, shredding pieces of flesh from the prey.

SIZE 60–70 cm (23.5–28 in)

HABITAT Continental shelves up to at least 100 m (328 ft) deep

DISTRIBUTION Northeastern and eastern Atlantic Ocean

·loudy catshark

·cyliorhinus torazame

One of the few shark species to be successfully bred in captivity, the cloudy catshark is often found in aquariums. It is a bottom-dweller, found among rocky reefs. It migrates only short distances.

SIZE 48 cm (19 in)

HABITAT Continental shelves up to at least 320 m (1,050 ft) deep

DISTRIBUTION Northwestern and western central Pacific Ocean

SMALLSPOTTED CATSHARK EGGS
The smallspotted catshark is an oviparous species that lays eggs in shallow waters near coasts and reefs. Also known as mermaid's purses, the eggs have tendrils that wrap around rocks and seaweed, anchoring the eggs in place.

A mermaid's purse

shark egg can remain attached to a rock for up to 11 months while the embryo grows inside

Soupfin shark
Galeorhinus galeus

Also known as the tope, school, or snapper shark, this fish is found in cool to subtropical seas around much of the world. The soupfin shark is slow to mature and is at risk of being overfished.

SIZE 1.2–1.9 m (4–6.25 ft)

HABITAT Continental shelves and slopes up to 500 m (1,640 ft) deep

DISTRIBUTION Southwestern and eastern Atlantic Ocean, western and eastern Indian Ocean, and western and eastern Pacific Ocean

Brown smoothhound
Mustelus henlei

This small, slender shark is a fast-growing species. It swims actively when kept in an aquarium and is one of the most successful sharks to be bred in captivity. It gives birth to 3–5 pups in a litter.

SIZE 0.5–1 m (1.5–3.3 ft)

HABITAT Continental shelves up to 200 m (656 ft) deep

DISTRIBUTION Eastern Pacific Ocean

Starry smoothhound
Mustelus asterias

An ovoviviparous species, the starry smoothhound gives birth to a litter of 7–15 pups after a 12-month gestation period. Although it spends most of its time away from the coast, many starry smoothhounds migrate to pupping grounds near the shore during summer.

SIZE 0.8–1.5 m (2.5–5 ft)

HABITAT Continental shelves up to 200 m (656 ft) deep

DISTRIBUTION Northeastern Atlantic Ocean

Leopard shark

Triakis semifasciata

Saddle-shaped pattern on the back

The leopard shark lives in oxygen-poor waters, where there is less competition for food, and preys on shrimp and fish eggs. It absorbs oxygen more efficiently than other sharks because its red blood cells, which carry oxygen in the bloodstream, are smaller and more numerous.

SIZE 1–2.1 m (3.3–7 ft)

HABITAT Continental shelves up to 50 m (164 ft) deep

DISTRIBUTION Northeastern, eastern, and central Pacific Ocean

Spotted estuary smoothhound
Mustelus lenticulatus

This shark is a highly migratory species. Males, females, and sharks of the same size form separate schools (groups). Also known as the rig shark or lemonfish, its meat is served in fish and chip shops in New Zealand.

SIZE 0.85–1.5 m (2.75–5 ft)

HABITAT Continental shelves and beyond up to 860 m (2,820 ft) deep

DISTRIBUTION Waters around New Zealand

Whiskery shark
Furgaleus macki

During the 1970s, the whiskery shark was heavily fished in Australia for its meat, leading to a 70 per cent decrease in population. Strict conservation measures by the Australian government have allowed the population to grow back.

SIZE 1.1–1.5 m (3.5–5 ft)

HABITAT Continental shelves up to 220 m (720 ft) deep

DISTRIBUTION Eastern Indian Ocean, near southern Australia

Snaggletooth shark
Hemipristis elongatus

Despite its hooked and dangerous-looking teeth, the snaggletooth is harmless to humans.

This shark gets its name from its jagged, sawlike teeth. The lower teeth protrude outwards even when its mouth is closed. It meat and liver, which is a rich source of vitamins, are sold for human consumption.

SIZE 1.1–2.4 m (3.5–8 ft)

HABITAT Continental shelves up to 130 m (427 ft) deep

DISTRIBUTION Indian Ocean and western Pacific Ocean

Hooktooth shark

Chaenogaleus macrostoma

This shark is fished for food by humans and its byproducts are processed into fishmeal. It feeds on small fish and crustaceans. This viviparous species gives birth to four pups per litter.

SIZE 0.8–1.25 m (2.5–4 ft)

HABITAT Continental shelves up to at least 59 m (194 ft) deep

DISTRIBUTION Indian Ocean and northwestern and western central Pacific Ocean

Sicklefin weasel shark

Hemigaleus microstoma

Found in shallow waters, this shark feeds mainly on octopuses and crustaceans. The sicklefin weasel shark may be under threat from overfishing in some localities.

SIZE 0.6–1.1 m (2–3.5 ft)

HABITAT Continental shelves up to 170 m (558 ft) deep

DISTRIBUTION Indian Ocean and northwestern and western central Pacific Ocean

Spinner shark
Carcharhinus brevipinna

The spinner shark gets its name from its actions when hunting. It sometimes charges through a school of fish from below, spinning through the air as it does so.

SIZE 1.6–2.8 m (5.25–9 ft)

HABITAT Coastal waters and offshore up to 100 m (328 ft) deep

DISTRIBUTION Western and eastern Atlantic Ocean, western Pacific Ocean, and western and eastern Indian Ocean

Galápagos shark
Carcharhinus galapagensis

The Galápagos shark lives and hunts around oceanic islands, sometimes swimming long distances from one island to another in search of prey. It can often be seen in schools around seamounts (mountains submerged in water).

SIZE 1.7–3.7 m (5.5–12 ft)

HABITAT Around oceanic islands in waters up to 180 m (590 ft) deep

DISTRIBUTION Western and eastern Atlantic Ocean, western Indian Ocean, and western, central, and eastern Pacific Ocean

Silky shark
Carcharhinus falciformis

Newborn silky sharks spend their early months in sheltered reefs. As they grow older, they begi venturing out into open waters, moving in grouŗ for protection. A keen sense of hearing helps them detect even the slightest noise made by their prey.

SIZE 2–3 m (6.5–10 ft)

HABITAT Open oceans up to 500 m (1,640 ft) deep

DISTRIBUTION Atlantic Ocean, Indian Ocean, and Pacific Ocean

Silvertip shark

Carcharhinus albimarginatus

The silvertip shark has an unusual method of defence when threatened by a rival or predator. The shark first swims away to a distance of 15 m (49 ft) and then moves rapidly towards the threat. Once it is about 3.5 m (11.5 ft) away, it stops, turns to its side, and shivers, displaying the white markings on its fins as a warning to back off. If the rival or predator does not move away, the shark closes in and may slash it with its teeth.

SIZE 2–2.5 m (6.5–8.25 ft)

HABITAT Continental shelves and beyond up to 800 m (2,625 ft) deep

DISTRIBUTION Western Indian Ocean and western, central, and eastern Pacific Ocean

Narrowly rounded or pointed fin with a white tip

BRONZE WHALER SHARK
From May to July, billions of sardines migrate in masses up to 7 km (4.3 miles) long, which act as the perfect larder for the bronze whaler. Bony fish such as sardines make up the main part of this predator's diet, along with squid and small sharks.

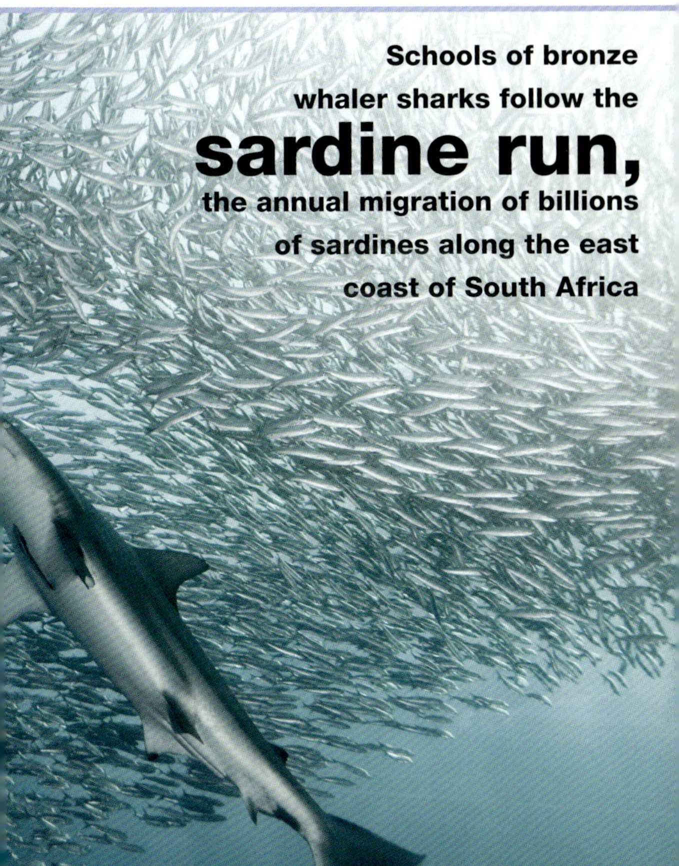

Schools of bronze whaler sharks follow the

sardine run,

the annual migration of billions of sardines along the east coast of South Africa

Blue shark
Prionace glauca

The blue shark is most active during the evening and at night. It is probably the most heavily fished shark in the world and is caught mainly for its fins. It is highly migratory, travelling long distances in search of food and to mate.

SIZE Up to 3.3–4 m (11–13 ft)

HABITAT Continental shelves and beyond up to 350 m (1,150 ft) deep

DISTRIBUTION Atlantic Ocean, Indian Ocean, and Pacific Ocean

Oceanic whitetip shark
Cacharhinus longimanus

Although it usually hunts alone, the oceanic whitetip shark can form groups where plenty of food is available. When competing with other species of shark for food, it becomes aggressive towards them. It is known to follow ships and can be dangerous to humans.

SIZE Up to 3.75 m (12.3 ft)

HABITAT Open oceans up to 200 m (656 ft) deep

DISTRIBUTION Atlantic Ocean, Indian Ocean, and Pacific Ocean

usky shark

archarhinus obscurus

e dusky shark matures slowly, with nales only breeding when they are at st 15 years old. They then mate every her year. Slow breeding puts them at k of overfishing.

SIZE 3.4–4 m (11.2–13 ft)

HABITAT Continental shelves and beyond up to 400 m (1,310 ft) deep

DISTRIBUTION Western and eastern Atlantic Ocean, Indian Ocean, and western and eastern Pacific Ocean

Sandbar shark
Carcharhinus plumbeus

The sandbar shark is one of the world's largest coastal sharks. It is hunted for its meat, leather, and oil.

SIZE 2–2.5 m (6.5–8.25 ft)

HABITAT Continental shelves and beyond up to 280 m (920 ft) deep

DISTRIBUTION Warm waters of the Atlantic Ocean, Indian Ocean, and Pacific Ocean

Blacknose shark
Carcharhinus acronotus

This small, schooling shark gets its name from the black blotch found on the tip of its snout. A fast, agile swimmer, the blacknose shark's speed sometimes allows it to snatch food from bigger sharks.

SIZE 1–2 m (3.3–6.5 ft)

HABITAT Continental shelves up to 64 m (210 ft) deep

DISTRIBUTION Western Atlantic Ocean

Sharptooth lemon shark
Negaprion acutidens

Though similar in appearance to the lemon shark, the sharptooth lemon shark can be recognized by its sickle-shaped pectoral fins. This shark is thought to be non-migratory, as it appears to remain in small areas throughout the year.

SIZE 2.2–3 m (7.2–10 ft)

HABITAT Rocky, sandy, or muddy sea beds up to 30 m (98 ft) deep

DISTRIBUTION Indian Ocean and western and central Pacific Ocean

·emon shark
legaprion brevirostris

'his is a stocky, powerful shark, named for s pale yellow-brown to grey skin. It does not ave any markings on its body, which allows to blend in perfectly with its coastal habitat.

IZE 2–3 m (6.5–10 ft)

ABITAT Coastal waters up to 90 m 295 ft) deep

ISTRIBUTION Western and eastern Atlantic Ocean

Tiger shark
Galeocerdo cuvier

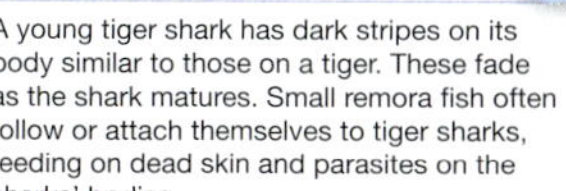

A young tiger shark has dark stripes on its body similar to those on a tiger. These fade as the shark matures. Small remora fish often follow or attach themselves to tiger sharks, feeding on dead skin and parasites on the sharks' bodies.

SIZE 4–6.5 m (13–21.5 ft)

HABITAT Coastal and offshore waters up to 140 m (459 ft) deep

DISTRIBUTION Warm waters of the Atlantic Ocean, Indian Ocean, and Pacific Ocean

Young lemon sharks can lose a **whole set of teeth,** one by one, every 10 days. A tooth from the row behind moves forwards to fill the gap

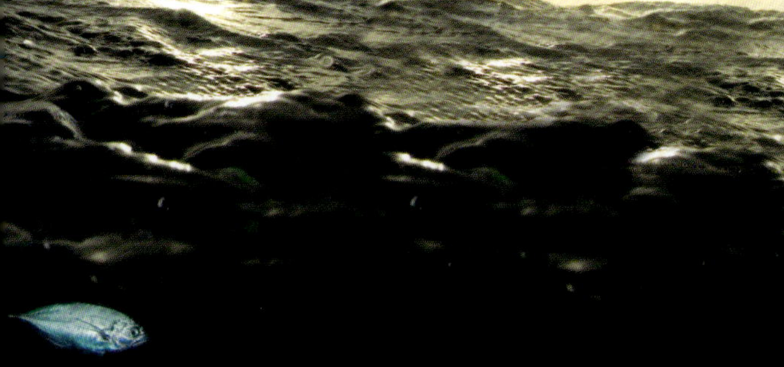

LEMON SHARK

Female lemon sharks give birth to up to 17 pups, and leave them to fend for themselves as soon as they are born. The young sharks stay in shallow nursery waters for several years until they are large enough to swim further offshore to find their own mates.

Grey reef shark

Carcharhinus amblyrhynchos

The grey reef shark shows a warning behaviour before attacking a potential threat – it assumes a hunched posture by lowering its pectoral fins and begins swimming from side to side. Although these sharks are not very big, their aggressive nature enables them to ward off most larger sharks.

SIZE 1.2–1.9 m (4–6.25 ft)

HABITAT Inshore, offshore, and oceanic waters up to 140 m (459 ft) deep

DISTRIBUTION Indian Ocean and western and central Pacific Ocean

Caribbean reef shark

Carcharhinus perezi

During the day, this shark will sometimes rest for short periods under ledges or in caves. When swimming near coral reefs, they are a popular spectacle for divers.

SIZE 2–2.95 m (6.5–9.75 ft)

HABITAT Continental shelves up to 30 m (98 ft) deep

DISTRIBUTION Western Atlantic Ocean

Blacktip reef shark
Carcharhinus melanopterus

The prominent black-tipped fins and light brown to grey upper body of the blacktip reef shark make it easily recognizable. This timid shark rarely poses a danger to humans.

SIZE Up to 1.6 m (5.25 ft)

HABITAT Coral reefs up to 10 m (33 ft) deep

DISTRIBUTION Indian Ocean, central and western Pacific Ocean, and part of the Mediterranean Sea

Bull shark
Carcharhinus leucas

The bull shark is found across the world, not only in oceans but in rivers as well. It is usually a solitary creature and aggressively attacks any animal that enters its territory.

SIZE 3–3.4 m (10–11.2 ft)

HABITAT Coastal waters up to 152 m (500 ft) deep and in freshwater rivers and lakes

DISTRIBUTION Warm waters of the Atlantic Ocean, Indian Ocean, and Pacific Ocean and some rivers and lakes

Great hammerhead

Sphyrna mokarran

This shark is the largest hammerhead species. The strange shape of its head helps the great hammerhead find buried stingrays, its favourite prey. Swinging its head from side to side, this shark uses its electrical sense to locate the stingray, pin the ray down with its head, twist the ray around, and bite.

SIZE Up to 6.1 m (20 ft)

HABITAT Coastal, offshore, and oceanic waters up to 80 m (262 ft) deep

DISTRIBUTION Tropical waters of the Atlantic Ocean, Indian Ocean, and Pacific Ocean

Scalloped hammerhead

Sphyrna lewini

ENDANGERED

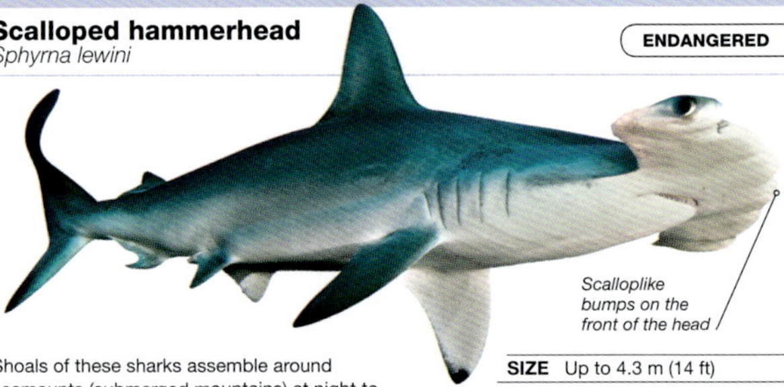

Scalloplike bumps on the front of the head

Shoals of these sharks assemble around seamounts (submerged mountains) at night to feed on sleeping or schooling fish. Its population has been severely affected by overfishing due to the growing demand for its fins.

SIZE Up to 4.3 m (14 ft)

HABITAT Coastal waters and beyond up to 275 m (900 ft) deep

DISTRIBUTION Warm waters of the Atlantic Ocean, Indian Ocean, and Pacific Ocean

Bonnethead shark
Sphyrna tiburo

The head of a bonnethead shark is shaped more like a shovel than a hammer. This allows it to dig out crabs and shellfish.

SIZE Up to 1.5 m (5 ft)

HABITAT Coastal waters up to 80 m (262 ft) deep

DISTRIBUTION Western Atlantic Ocean and eastern Pacific Ocean

Winghead shark
Eusphyra blochii

Long and narrow head blades, known as cephalofoils, give this shark a unique appearance. It feeds on fish, crustaceans, octopuses, and squid.

SIZE Up to 1.8 m (6 ft)

HABITAT Shallow, coastal waters

DISTRIBUTION Northern and eastern Indian Ocean and western Pacific Ocean

Smooth hammerhead
Sphyrna zygaena

The third-largest hammerhead species, the smooth hammerhead is a fearsome predator. It feeds on bony fish, rays, sharks, and squid. It is actively hunted for its fins, which are used to make shark fin soup.

SIZE Up to 4 m (13 ft)

HABITAT Coastal and offshore waters up to at least 20 m (66 ft) deep

DISTRIBUTION Temperate to warm waters of the Atlantic Ocean, Indian Ocean, and Pacific Ocean

Scalloped hammerheads can form schools of up to

500 sharks

SCALLOPED HAMMERHEAD
Unlike most shark species, scalloped hammerheads form schools, often near seamounts, where there is a good supply of food. The largest females swim in the centre of a school, which is where males head to find a mate. Males prefer larger females because they produce more pups than smaller females.

Rays, skates, and chimaeras

Like their shark relatives, rays, skates, sawfish, and chimaeras are cartilaginous fish. Rays and skates have flat bodies, with broad winglike fins. Some of them, such as the stingray (left), have sharp stings on their tail, which are used for defence. One family of rays, the sawfish, use their heads rather than their tails for defence. Their long snouts are edged with sharp, toothlike denticles that are ideal for slashing prey as well as defending against attackers.

CHIMAERAS
Found in deep water, chimaeras are also known as rabbitfish because their front cutting teeth and back grinding teeth resemble those of a rabbit.

Shark relatives

Skates, rays, and sawfish can be grouped together in one superorder called Batoidea, with more than 600 species divided into six orders. These fish are close relatives of sharks, and share many features with them, including a skeleton made of cartilage. The final group of cartilaginous fish is the chimaeras, which are more distantly related to sharks and skates.

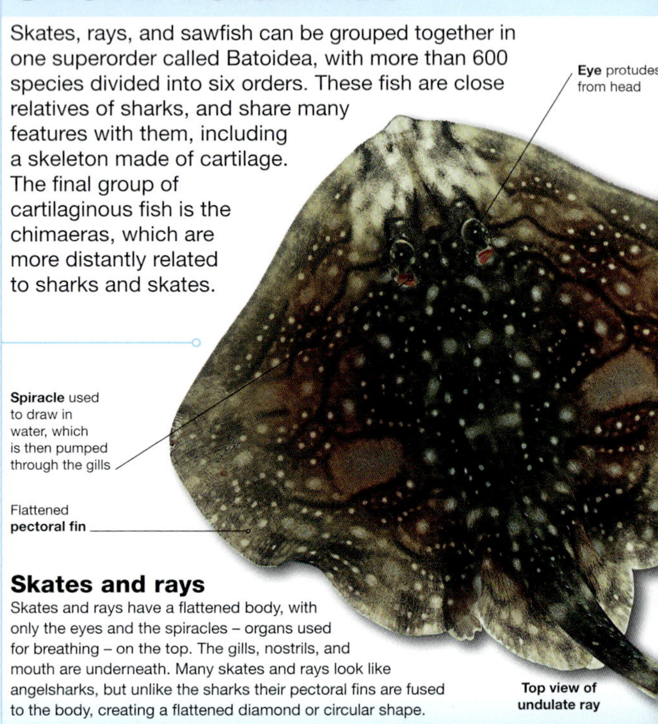

Skates and rays

Skates and rays have a flattened body, with only the eyes and the spiracles – organs used for breathing – on the top. The gills, nostrils, and mouth are underneath. Many skates and rays look like angelsharks, but unlike the sharks their pectoral fins are fused to the body, creating a flattened diamond or circular shape.

Top view of undulate ray

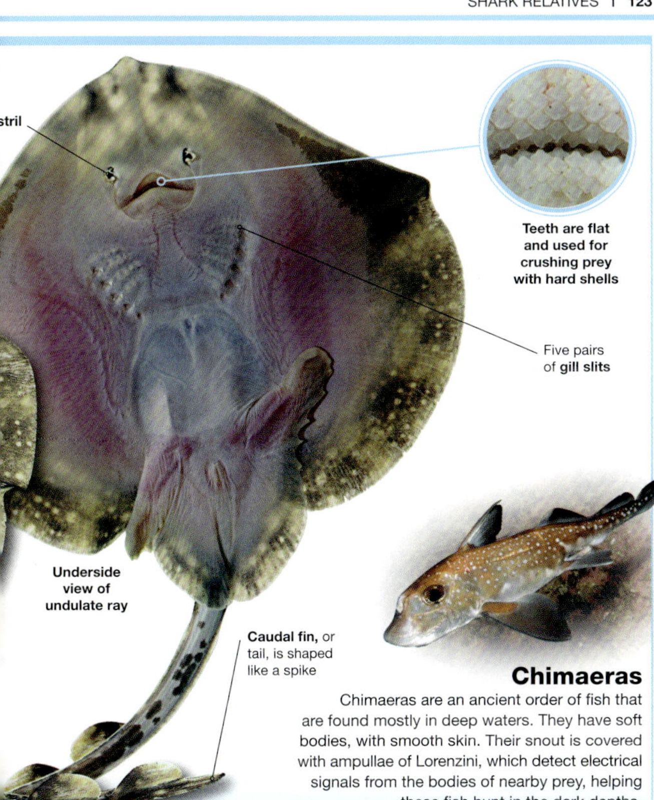

Chimaeras

Chimaeras are an ancient order of fish that are found mostly in deep waters. They have soft bodies, with smooth skin. Their snout is covered with ampullae of Lorenzini, which detect electrical signals from the bodies of nearby prey, helping these fish hunt in the dark depths.

Sawfish

Sawfish resemble sawsharks, but are much bigger in size and do not have barbels. All species are endangered – they are slow to reproduce and they get easily entangled in fishing nets.

FOCUS ON...
FEATURES

A number of features distinguish sawfish from sawsharks.

▲ Sawfish have gills on the underside of the body, while sawsharks have gills on the sides.

▲ The mouth of a sawfish is on the underside of its body. In a sawshark, it is more towards the front of its head.

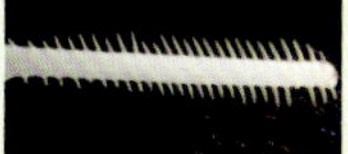

▲ Both sawsharks and sawfish have teeth on either side of the snout, but in sawsharks the teeth are more uneven in length.

Largetooth sawfish

Pristis microdon

ENDANGERED

The long denticles on its snout gives the largetooth sawfish its name. Despite its fearsome appearance, the fish does not attack humans unless provoked or taken by surprise. This shark is being overfished for its meat and so its populations are under threat.

SIZE 5–7 m (16.5–23 ft)

HABITAT Rivers, freshwater lakes, and coastal waters up to 10 m (33 ft) deep

DISTRIBUTION Rivers and lakes of southeastern Asia, Australia, and southeastern Africa and nearby coastal waters

Narrowsnout sawfish

Pristis zijsron

ENDANGERED

This species is the largest of all the sawfish. Like all sawfish, this species keeps its body flat on the sea bed but holds its snout upwards at an angle while resting. It sleeps during the day and hunts at night, stunning its prey with a sideways swipe of the snout.

SIZE 7.3 m (24 ft)

HABITAT Rivers, freshwater lakes, and coastal waters up to 40 m (131 ft) deep

DISTRIBUTION Indian Ocean, western Pacific Ocean, and rivers and lakes in South Africa and northern New Zealand

Knifetooth sawfish

Anoxypristis cuspidata

ENDANGERED

All teeth are of the same length

The knifetooth sawfish has a narrow snout with 18–22 pairs of daggerlike teeth on it. The skin of the juveniles is smooth, but adults grow thornlike scales on their skin. Like other sawfish, when caught it is known to thrash about violently, and it may injure fishermen.

SIZE 4.7 m (15.5 ft)

HABITAT Rivers, freshwater lakes, and coastal waters up to 40 m (131 ft) deep

DISTRIBUTION Indian Ocean and western Pacific Ocean

Guitarfish

About 50 species of guitarfish have been identified, and they belong in two orders: Rhinobatiformes and Rhiniformes. These creatures have raylike fins, but their hind body is narrower like a shark.

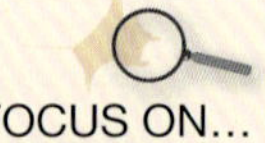

FOCUS ON...
SHAPE
Guitarfish are named for their unique body shape, which resembl the musical instrumer

Thornback guitarfish
Platyrhinoidis triseriata

This guitarfish has three parallel rows of large, hooked thorns that run from the middle of its back to its tail. Like sharks and other rays, guitarfish have ampullae of Lorenzini on their snouts, which help them detect electrical signals produced by prey.

SIZE 37–90 cm (14.5–35 in)
HABITAT Coastal waters up to 137 m (450 ft) deep
DISTRIBUTION Eastern Pacific Ocean

Atlantic guitarfish
Rhinobatos lentiginosus

Also known as the freckled guitarfish, the Atlant guitarfish is the smallest member of its order. The upper part of its body is covered with freckles while its belly is a pale yellow.

SIZE Up to 76 cm (30 in)
HABITAT Coastal waters up to 30 m (98 ft) de
DISTRIBUTION Western Atlantic Ocean

. These fish have a triangular body shape, ith a pointed snout, broad pectoral fins, ıd a long tapering tail end.

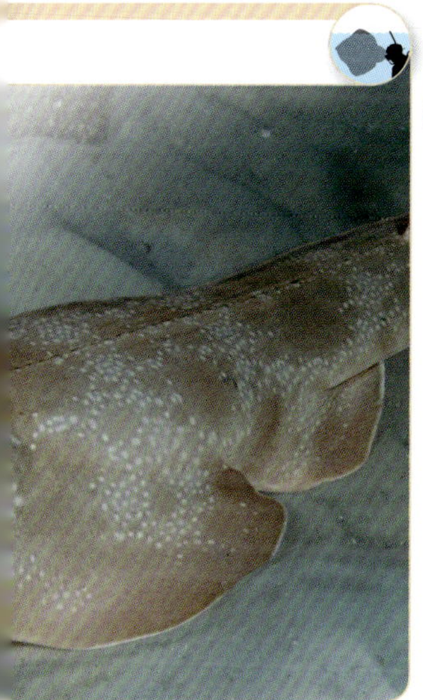

Common guitarfish
Rhinobatos rhinobatos

This fish hunts its prey either by swimming slowly along the bottom of the sea bed or lying partially buried in sand and ambushing prey. The common guitarfish feeds on shrimp, crabs, and small fish.

SIZE 0.75–1.7 m (2.5–5.5 ft)

HABITAT Coastal waters up to 180 m (590 ft) deep

DISTRIBUTION Eastern Atlantic Ocean, Mediterranean Sea, and Black Sea

Skates

Skates are a particular kind of ray that have a kite-shaped, flattened body and winglike pectoral fins. They belong to the order Rajiformes. There are more than 200 species of skate, but many of them are at risk of becoming endangered due to overfishing for their meat and the destruction of their habitats.

Big skate

Raja binoculata

This fish is the largest skate in North America. Raised, pointed denticles (or thorns) are present on the upper surface of the adult's body, while the young have a smoother skin. This skate usually lies hidden in sand, with only its eyes exposed.

SIZE 1–2.4 m (3.3–8 ft)

HABITAT Continental shelves up to 200 m (656 ft) deep

DISTRIBUTION Northeastern Pacific Ocean

Thornback skate

Raja clavata

This skate is called a thornback skate because of the three rows of small, sharp thorns on its back and tail. It feeds on small, bottom-dwelling animals such as worms, crabs, and fish.

SIZE 1–1.3 m (3.3–4.25 ft)

HABITAT Coastal reefs up to 300 m (984 ft) deep

DISTRIBUTION Northern and eastern Atlantic Ocean, Mediterranean Sea, and Black Sea

Undulate ray
Raja undulata

ENDANGERED

Although it is called the undulate ray, this species is actually a skate. The upper surface of its body has a vivid pattern of wavy brown stripes dotted with white and yellow spots. This helps it blend in with the sandy sea bed on which it lives.

SIZE 1 m (3.3 ft)

HABITAT Continental shelves up to 200 m (656 ft) depth

DISTRIBUTION Northeastern and eastern central Atlantic Ocean

Common skate ENDANGERED
Dipturus batis

The common skate is the largest skate species. It feeds on bottom-dwelling crustaceans, shellfish, and fish. This skate envelops its prey in its pectoral fins before capturing and eating it.

SIZE 1–2.9 m (3.3–9.5 ft)

HABITAT Coastal waters up to 600 m (1,970 ft) deep

DISTRIBUTION Northeastern and eastern Atlantic Ocean

Thorny skate
Amblyraja radiata

This skate has a very rough upper body surface, with small thorns scattered all over its disc and tail. The thorny skate also has a distinct black spot on the tip of its tail.

SIZE Up to 1.05 m (3.4 ft)

HABITAT Continental shelves and beyond up to 1,000 m (3,280 ft) deep

DISTRIBUTION Northeastern and northwestern Atlantic Ocean

Australian thornback skate
Dentiraja lemprieri

The Australian thornback skate is a slow swimm and often lies motionless on the sea bed. It feeds on crabs, shrimp, lobsters, and other small, bottom-dwelling animals, including fish. The female is larger than the male and lays dozens of eggs in a breeding season.

ZE 55 cm (21.5 in)

ABITAT Continental shelves up to 170 m
58 ft) deep

STRIBUTION Southwestern Pacific Ocean
d eastern Indian Ocean, around Tasmania

The Australian thornback skate has spines along its back, giving it extra protection.

Peacock skate

Pavoraja nitida

The peacock skate has a prominent black patch on the lower side of its snout tip. The young skates can often be seen following their mother.

SIZE Up to 37 cm (14.5 in)

HABITAT Continental shelves and beyond up to 390 m (1,280 ft) deep

DISTRIBUTION Southwestern Pacific Ocean and eastern Indian Ocean

Little skate

Leucoraja erinacea

The little skate is more active at night and in dark conditions. Its tail contains an electric organ, which is thought to help it communicate with other skates and detect potential mates.

SIZE Up to 54 cm (21.25 in)

HABITAT Continental shelves and beyond up to 330 m (1,080 ft) deep

DISTRIBUTION Northwestern Atlantic Ocean

Electric rays

Electric rays have special organs in their bodies that produce an electrical current, which can reach 220 volts in the largest species. They use this both to stun prey and in defence. The best-known member of this family is the torpedo ray, which inspired the name of the torpedo weapon.

Giant electric ray

Narcine entemedor

The giant electric ray, also known as the Cortez electric ray, feeds at night and spends the day lying half-buried in sand. While searching for food, it glides along the sea bed using its flexible fins.

SIZE Up to 93 cm (36.5 in)

HABITAT Sandy sea beds up to 100 m (328 ft) deep

DISTRIBUTION Eastern and southeastern Pacific Ocean

Ocellated electric ray

Diplobatis ommata

This electric ray is easily recognized by the bullseye pattern on its back. It feeds on small fish, crabs, shrimp, and small worms. This solitary creature is capable of generating a painful electric shock in self defence.

SIZE Up to 25 cm (10 in)

HABITAT Rocky reefs up to 94 m (308 ft) deep

DISTRIBUTION Eastern Pacific Ocean

Marbled electric ray

orpedo marmorata

ne marbled ectric ray, or potted electric ray, is slow-moving predator at attacks its prey from elow, capturing its victims after unning them with strong electric shocks.

IZE 21–61 cm (8.5–24 in)

ABITAT Sandy, stony, or rocky a beds up to 100 m (328 ft) deep

STRIBUTION Eastern Atlantic Ocean d Mediterranean Sea

Common torpedo
Torpedo torpedo

The common torpedo can discharge 200 volts – enough to give a person a severe shock.

The common torpedo is easily identified by the large blue "eye-spots" on the upper surface of its body. These spots vary between five and nine in number. The female of this viviparous species can give birth to up to 28 young at a time.

SIZE 30–40 cm (12–16 in)

HABITAT Warm waters up to 300 m (984 ft) deep

DISTRIBUTION Eastern Atlantic Ocean and Mediterranean Sea

Black-spotted torpedo

Torpedo fuscomaculata

A lesser-known ray, this torpedo is confined mostly to the waters near southern Africa. It feeds on cuttlefish and a variety of small fish, including sea bream and beaked sandfish.

SIZE Up to 64 cm (25 in)

HABITAT Continental shelves and beyond up to 440 m (1,440 ft) deep

DISTRIBUTION Southeastern Atlantic Ocean and western Indian Ocean

Stingrays

Stingrays belong to the order Myliobatiformes. Their popular name comes from the one or more venomous stings on their tail. However, not all stingrays have stings. Most do, including the four whiptail stingrays on these pages, but butterfly rays and manta rays do not.

Common stingray

Dasyatis pastinaca

Humans have been familiar with the common stingray since ancient times. The venom in its sting was once considered to have no cure and even turn iron to rust. However, although its sting can cause a very painful wound, it is not usually fatal to humans.

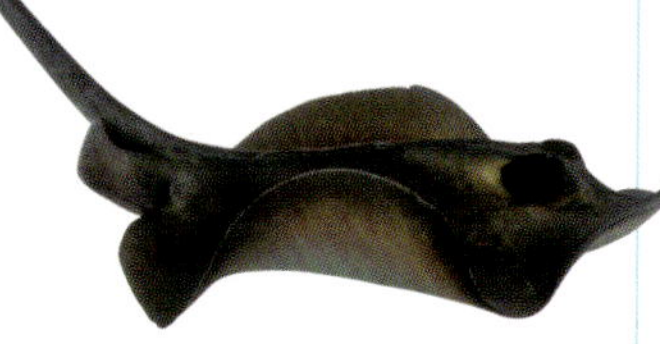

SIZE 0.3–2.5 m (1–8.25 ft)

HABITAT Continental shelves up to 200 m (656 ft) deep

DISTRIBUTION Northeastern Atlantic Ocean, Mediterranean Sea, and Black Sea

Leopard stingray

Himantura uarnak

Also called the reticulate whipray, this fish gets its name from the pattern on the upper surface of its body, which resembles a leopard's skin. This species hunts at night and spends most of the daytime lying still on the sea bed.

SIZE Up to 2 m (6.5 ft)

HABITAT Sea beds up to 50 m (164 ft) deep

DISTRIBUTION Indian Ocean and western Pacific Ocean

'OCUS ON... 'AIL

'pecies in the family f whiptail stingrays ave a tail that is nger than the body.

▼ A whiptail's main defence is its tail. It has up to three stings, which are used to inject predators with venom produced by a gland below the sting.

Southern stingray

Dasyatis americana

'his stingray finds its food by flapping its fins ver the sea bed to expose crabs and other rustaceans hidden beneath. This docile creature ses its long, barbed whiplike tail only in defence.

IZE Up to 2.5 m (8.25 ft)

ABITAT Sea beds up to 53 m (174 ft) deep

ISTRIBUTION Western Atlantic Ocean, ulf of Mexico, and Caribbean Sea

Ribbontail stingray

Taeniura lymma

This stingray spends most of its time near rocky and coral reefs. However, when the water level rises during high tide, it moves into shallow lagoons. It feeds on shrimp, small fish, crabs, and worms.

SIZE 70–90 cm (28–35 in)

HABITAT Coral and rocky reefs and nearby sandflats up to 25 m (82 ft) deep

DISTRIBUTION Indian Ocean and western Pacific Ocean

Cowtail stingray
Pastinachus sephen

This fish can easily be recognized by the large flaglike fold on its tail. The cowtail stingray is threatened from overfishing because its skin is used to make shagreen, a high-quality leather.

SIZE 1.4–3 m (4.5–10 ft)

HABITAT Coral reefs, rocky or sandy sea beds, and rivers up to 60 m (197 ft) deep

DISTRIBUTION Indian Ocean and western Pacific Ocean

Round stingray
Urobatis halleri

As in some other stingray species, the main spine on the tail of the round stingray is periodically shed. Early in the year, round stingrays have one spine on the tail. By summer, a second spine grows. By winter, the original spine falls off and the second spine replaces it. These stingrays are found in warm waters above 10°C (50°F).

SIZE Up to 45 cm (18 in)

HABITAT Muddy or sandy sea beds up to 90 m (295 ft) deep

DISTRIBUTION Eastern Pacific Ocean

Spiny butterfly ray
Gymnura altavela

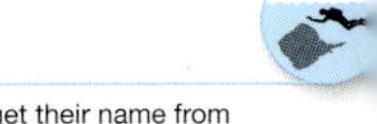

Butterfly rays get their name from their elongated “wings” (pectoral fins). These disturb the sand as it swims, uncovering small prey such as fish and snails, which the ray scoops up in its mouth.

SIZE 2–3 m (6.5–10 ft)

HABITAT Sandy sea beds up to 55 m (180 ft) deep

DISTRIBUTION Western and eastern Atlantic Ocean and Mediterranean Sea

Ocellate stingray
Potamotrygon motoro

This freshwater stingray's name means "bearing eyelike spots", and it is also known as the peacock-eye stingray. Newborn rays prey on plankton, but as they grow up, they start feeding on molluscs, crustaceans, and the larvae of water insects.

SIZE Up to 90 cm (35 in)

HABITAT Freshwater

DISTRIBUTION Several rivers in South America

Eye raised above body surface

Spotted eagle ray
Aetobatus narinari

The spotted eagle ray swims by beating its pectoral fins in a similar way to a bird flapping its wings. In open waters, these fish often form large schools and swim close to the surface. Its attractive dorsal spots make it a favourite at public aquariums.

SIZE 1–4 m (3.3–13 ft)

HABITAT Continental shelves up to 60 m (200 ft) deep

DISTRIBUTION Western and eastern Atlantic Ocean, Indian Ocean, and western, central, and eastern Pacific Ocean

The spotted eagle ray can leap clear out of the water to escape predators.

Giant manta ray
Manta birostris

A filter feeder, the giant manta ray feeds by pulling in water through its mouth and passing the water through its gills. Special organs on its gills, called gill rakers, strain the plankton out of the water. An average-sized manta eats up to 30 kg (66 lb) of plankton in a single day.

SIZE 4.5–9 m (14.75–30 ft)

HABITAT Near coral and rocky reefs up to 120 m (390 ft) deep

DISTRIBUTION Atlantic Ocean, Pacific Ocean, and Indian Ocean

Javanese cownose ray
Rhinoptera javanica

This unusual-looking ray has an indented forehead and a double-lobed snout, which looks like a flap. It has a kite-shaped body, which is brown on top and white below. Its long tail is armed with one or more stings.

SIZE 1–1.5 m (3.3–5 ft)

HABITAT Coastal waters up to 30 m (100 ft) deep

DISTRIBUTION Indian Ocean and western Pacific Ocean

MANTA RAY
Manta rays are sometimes called devil rays because of the "horns" projecting from their head. When they feed, they unfurl these fleshy lobes, which direct water into the mouth. They strain out plankton from the water using spongy tissue in their gills.

The largest species of ray, the giant manta ray can grow up to

9 m (30 ft)

across from the tip of one fin to the other

Chimaeras

Although chimaeras and sharks share a common ancestor, the chimaeras began evolving separately from the sharks around 400 million years ago. These fish have a large head and their teeth are arranged like those in a rabbit's mouth, with teeth for grabbing and slicing at the front and teeth for grinding at the back.

Spotted ratfish

Hydrolagus colliei

The spotted ratfish is so named because its tail resembles that of a rat. The dorsal fin of this fish has a venomous spine, which is used in defence. A strong sense of smell allows it to locate prey easily, such as crabs, clams, and small fish.

SIZE 60 cm (23.5 in)

HABITAT Coastal waters and continental slopes up to 900 m (2,950 ft) deep

DISTRIBUTION Northeastern and eastern Pacific Ocean

Knifenose chimaera

Rhinochimaera pacifica

Also known as the Pacific spookfish, this chimaera is named for its long, conical snout. The snout is covered with sensory pores that help it detect prey, most likely through a combination of smell and vibration.

SIZE Up to 1.3 m (4.25 ft)

HABITAT Offshore up to 1,300 m (4,265 ft) deep

DISTRIBUTION Western, southwestern, and southeastern Pacific Ocean and eastern Indian Ocean

Elephant fish

Callorhinchus milii

This chimaera has a long, fleshy snout that resembles an elephant's trunk, which it uses to sense and unearth shellfish from muddy sea beds. It also has a spine in front of its dorsal fin, which it uses to defend itself against predators.

SIZE 0.75–1.25 m (2.5–4 ft)

HABITAT Continental shelves up to 227 m (745 ft) deep

DISTRIBUTION Southwestern Pacific Ocean

Fascinating facts

SWIMMING AND MIGRATION

• **Sharks can't stop suddenly.** They must move left or right to avoid collisions. They also cannot swim backwards.

• **The fastest-moving shark** is the shortfin mako shark. It can reach speeds of more than 56 kph (35 mph).

• **Some large species of sharks undergo long migrations.** Atlantic blue sharks may do a round trip of up to 17,000 km (10,500 miles) in about 14 months, travelling between feeding grounds and breeding areas.

• **A great hammerhead shark** was recently tracked covering 1,200 km (745 miles) in 62 days.

• **Bull sharks** are the only common sharks that migrate from the salty oceans to rivers, travelling upstream to find food.

• **Perhaps the least enthusiastic traveller** is the nurse shark. It remains in an area of a few dozen square kilometres for its entire life.

In some sharks, the first embryo to develop eats the other embryos while still inside the mother. This is called oophagy.

LIFE CYCLE

▶ **Lemon sharks** can give birth to up to 17 pups in one litter.

▶ **Great hammerhead sharks** can give birth to up to 40 pups at once.

▶ **Whale sharks** can carry up to 300 embryos at a time. However, not all of these embryos hatch into pups.

▶ **Female sandbar sharks** start breedin when about 13 years old, but then only produce a few pups every two years.

▶ **Most sharks** live for 20 to 30 years, but some reach 80. Experts suspect that the large, slow whale shark may be capab of surviving for well over 100 years, makin it one of the longest-living animals on Eart

▶ **Some deepsea sharks** do not mature until they are at least 40 years old.

▶ **The liver** of a basking shark becomes even larger during pregnancy. This happe because the liver acts as a storehouse for energy that the shark needs during its 3-year-long pregnancy.

HUNTING AND FEEDING

A shark's ears are sensitive enough ɔ pick up sounds from several hundred ıetres away, helping it find prey easily.

Sharks have powerful jaws and ɔme sharks are capable of exerting) kg (132 lb) of pressure per tooth hen they bite.

Great white sharks may not eat r several days after a heavy meal.

Sharks living in cold water can heat eir eyes using a special organ next to a uscle in their eye socket. This lets them ınt in extreme temperatures.

Many sharks have a keen sense smell so powerful that they can detect single drop of blood in a bathtub of water.

DANGER

★ **Great white sharks** may be responsible for more attacks on people than any other species of shark. However, tiger and bull sharks also top the list of sharks that are known to attack humans.

★ **Second Beach** near Port St John's, South Africa, may be the most dangerous beach in the world. Between 2007 and 2012 at least one person each year was killed by a shark.

★ **Several dozen shark attacks** on humans are reported every year, while perhaps 100 million sharks are killed by humans each year.

★ **Apart from humans,** a shark's biggest enemy is another shark – many sharks are known to prey on members of their own or other shark species.

AYS AND RELATIVES

The green sawfish and giant anta ray are the biggest members of ə superorder Batoidea, growing to ɔre than 7.3 m (24 ft) long.

The giant manta ray is o the widest member of the / family – it can reach up to n (30 ft).

Some manta rays leap out of the water apparently for fun, jumping forward and landing head-first or tail-first and even doing backflips.

▶ **The knifetooth sawfish** can give birth to up to 23 young.

▶ The wound caused by a **stingray's venom** can take more than a year to heal.

▶ **The venom** from the spine of a stingray was used by ancient Greek dentists as an anaesthetic.

Largest and smallest sharks

THE LARGEST

Sharks include the largest fish in the world. They are among the oceans' top predators, feeding on fish, crustaceans, seals, and even dolphins and whales. Here are some of the longest sharks and their recorded lengths.

⑩ Bigeye thresher shark
This shark grows to a maximum length of 4.6 m (15 ft), with its tail accounting for about half of this length.

❾ Bluntnose sixgill shark or cow shark
The largest member of its family, this shark can reach a length of 4.8 m (15.75 ft).

❽ Thresher shark
Measured from the tip of the snout to the end of its tail, the thresher shark has a top length of 6 m (20 ft).

❼ Great hammerhead shark
The largest of all hammerhead species, the great hammerhead shark has been known to reach a length of 6.1 m (20 ft).

❻ Great white shark
Some female great whites can reach 6.4 m (21 ft). They are stockier and heavier than the tiger sharks, although they are about the same size.

❺ Tiger shark
The largest tiger sharks can grow to at least 6.5 m (21.5 ft) long.

❹ Pacific sleeper shark
This shark has a maximum recorded length of 7 m (23 ft).

❸ Greenland shark
A close relative of the Pacific sleeper shark, the Greenland shark can grow to a length of 7.3 m (24 ft).

❷ Basking shark
The basking shark reaches a maximum length of 12.3 m (40.4 ft).

❶ Whale shark
The whale shark is the largest shark in the world. The largest official record is 13.7 m (45 ft), but other reports claim lengths of up to 18 m (59 ft).

The two largest sharks in the world – the basking shark and whale shark – feed on tiny animal plankton.

HE SMALLEST

nese are some of the smallest sharks and their maximum corded adult lengths. Many small sharks live deep in the ocean nd are rarely seen. Working out to what length a species grows often based on just one or two individuals that have been aught accidentally.

Shorttail lanternshark
ving at depths of up to 480 m (1,575 ft), e shorttail lanternshark has a recorded aximum length of only 42 cm (16.5 in).

Longnose pygmy shark
ne rare longnose pygmy ark reaches a length of cm (14.5 in).

Granular dogfish
e granular dogfish has en found in two regions ar South America – the lkland Islands and Chile. grows to just over cm (11 in).

Spined pygmy catshark
male spined pygmy catsharks ach a length of 28 cm (11 in).

Thorny lanternshark
in most shark species, the female tures at a larger size than the male. e reaches up to 27 cm (10.5 in) long.

Sharks continue to grow throughout their lives, although the rate of growth slows down as they get older.

❺ Pygmy shark
The pygmy shark grows to just 27 cm (10.5 in) long.

❹ Green lanternshark
The green lanternshark reaches a maximum length of 26 cm (10 in).

❸ African lanternshark
This lanternshark can reach 24 cm (9.5 in) in length. It lives in the dark zone, some 1,000 m (3,280 ft) below the surface of the sea.

❷ Broadnose catshark
Only one broadnose catshark has ever been caught. It measured 24 cm (9.5 in) long.

❶ Dwarf lanternshark
Measuring up to 21 cm (8.5 in) in length, the dwarf lanternshark is probably the world's smallest shark.

GLOSSARY

Adaptation An evolutionary process that enables living things to fit their environment as well as possible.

Ampullae of Lorenzini Tiny sensors on the snout of a shark or a ray that help it pick up electrical signals from prey. Sharks and rays possibly use these sensors to sense Earth's magnetic field to help find their way.

Anal fin A fin located on the underside of the body in some sharks.

Anatomy The body structure of a life form or any of its parts.

Barbel A slender, whiskerlike organ, or feeler, found near the mouth of some sharks. It is used to search the sea bed for food.

Buoyancy The ability or tendency of an object or organism to float. Sharks have oil-filled livers to help their buoyancy.

Bycatch Sharks and other sea creatures that by chance get caught on baited lines or in fishing nets set for other fish.

Camouflage Colours or patterns that help an animal to blend in with its surroundings.

Carnivore An animal that eats only meat.

Cartilage A hard yet flexible tissue that forms the skeleton of cartilaginous fish. It is lighter and more flexible than bone.

Cartilaginous fish Fish that have skeletons made of cartilage rather than bone. They include sharks, skates, rays, and chimaeras.

Cavity A hollow area within an object or an organism.

Caudal fin The shark's tail. Sharks have caudal fins of many different shapes and sizes.

Conservation The process of protecting or preserving of animals and their habitats.

Continental shelf The part of the edge of a continent partially submerged in relatively shallow waters.

Continental slope A steep slope from a continental shelf to the ocean floor.

Crustacean A type of invertebrate with jointed legs. Crustaceans usually have hard outer shells. Copepods, krill, and crabs are examples of crustaceans.

Denticles Scales that cover a shark's skin. They are toothlike and dense and unlike those on bony fish. Denticles are made from the same minerals as teeth. They have different shapes depending on where they are on the shark's body. The ones on the snout are rounded, while those on the back are pointed.

Dorsal fin A large fin in the middle of a shark's back, which prevents it from rolling over. Some sharks also have a second, smaller dorsal fin near their tail.

Embryo An unborn animal that is developing inside its mother's womb or in an egg.

Enamel The outer coating of teeth. Enamel is the hardest substance in an animal's body.

Endangered species A species that is in danger of becoming extinct. Critically endangered species (such as Ganges sharks) are in immediate danger of dying out if existing conditions do not change.

Evolution The gradual change in living organisms that occurs over many generations.

Extinct A species that has died out. *Megalodon* sharks are extinct.

Feeler An organ, such as a tentacle or barbel, in some animals that helps them to touch or sense.

Filter feeder An animal that feeds by taking in large amounts of water that contains particles of food such as plankton which are then strained out of the water.

Finning Chopping fins off sharks to sell them. Often, the animal is thrown back into the sea, where it drowns as it can no longer swim.

Fossil The remains of an ancient animal or plant, preserved in rock.

Gestation The period between conception and birth in which a growing embryo is carried in the womb of the mother.

Gills Feathery structures in a shark's throat region that extract oxygen from the water, which is needed to help provide energy.

Gill rakers Projections like the teeth of a comb found in the gills of some fish, including sharks.

ıey strain tiny organisms ɔm the water that flows ver the gills.

ll slit An opening in the ıark's skin from which ater flows out. Most arks have five gill slits.

abitat The environment which an animal (or y life form) lives.

vertebrate An animal thout a backbone.

teral line A line cells along the sides of shark that are sensitive changes in water essure and can detect ɔvement in the water. is is useful for the ark in dark or ırky waters.

gration The process moving from one place another according to seasons, usually find food or to breed.

ctitating membrane special eyelid found in me animals and birds t is translucent or nsparent and helps protect the eye to keep it moist.

cturnal An animal that active at night.

iparous Producing js that hatch outside mother's body.

oviviparous Producing js that hatch inside mother's body.

Oxygen A gas that is found in air and water. Almost all living things need oxygen to survive.

Pectoral fin One of a pair of fins located under the front of a shark's body. The fish uses these to steer and generate lift in the water. They also act as brakes when necessary.

Pelagic Related to or living in the open ocean.

Pelvic fin One of a pair of fins located under the rear of a shark's body. These work with other fins to control swimming.

Plankton The mass of tiny plants and animals that float around in the sea and are eaten by many larger animals.

Predator An animal that hunts, kills, or eats other animals.

Prey An animal that is hunted, killed, or eaten by a predator.

Pup A baby shark.

Pupping ground An area where sharks gather to give birth.

Regurgitation The process in which an animal releases undigested food from its mouth.

Scavenger An animal that searches for food scraps, rather than hunting prey. Scavengers often eat the remains of animals killed by predators.

School A large group of fish swimming close together and moving as one. Also called a shoal.

Seamount An underwater mountain or volcano.

Shagreen The rough skin of many sharks and rays.

Snout The front part of a shark's head.

Species A group of plants or animals that share features and can breed only with one another.

Spiracles An extra pair of gill openings that supply oxygen to a shark's eyes and brain. Rays also use spiracles to pump water over their gills while they are resting on the sea bed.

Streamlined A smooth shape that is less resistant to air or water. Having a streamlined body helps a shark to swim faster.

Tagging A method of tracking and studying sharks in the wild, often by attaching computerized tags to their fins so their movements can be detected and recorded via a satellite.

Tapetum A layer of cells at the back of a shark's eye that reflects light, helping the fish to see clearly in the dark.

Temperate Mild weather or climate.

Tendril A slender armlike structure found in certain organisms. It is used to clasp prey or to move.

Tropical Hot and humid climate or weather as in the tropics.

Vertebrate An animal that has a backbone.

Vertical migration Movement of marine creatures from deep to shallow water or vice versa. Planktonic organisms migrate in this way daily, and they are often followed by sharks and other predators.

Viviparous Producing young that remain in the mother's body until they are fully formed and ready to be born.

Zoology The branch of science that deals with animals and animal life.

Index

OP

R

S

T

UV

WYZ

Acknowledgments

Dorling Kindersley would like to thank: Monica Byles for proofreading; Helen Peters for indexing; David Roberts and Rob Campbell for database creation; Claire Bowers, Fabian Harry, Romaine Werblow, and Rose Horridge for DK Picture Library assistance; Ritu Mishra, Jessica Cawthra, Priyanka Kharbanda, Vatsal Verma, Vicky Richards, Kingshuk Ghoshal, and Francesca Baines for editorial assistance; Isha Nagar, Chrissy Barnard, Ira Sharma, Kanupriya Lal, Govind Mittal, and Philip Letsu for design assistance; Saloni Singh for the jacket; Pawan Kumar and Balwant Singh for DTP assistance; Deepak Negi for picture research assistance; and Gillian Reid for pre-production.

The publishers would also like to thank the following for their kind permission to reproduce their photographs:

(Key: a-above; b-below/bottom; c-centre; f-far; l-left; r-right; t-top)

1 FLPA: ImageBroker (c). **2–3 Corbis:** Denis Scott (crb). **4–5 Getty Images:** Fleetham Dave / Perspectives (c). **6 marinethemes.com:** Kelvin Aitken (tl); Andy Murch (bl). **7 marinethemes.com:** Kelvin Aitken (cr). **8 Dorling Kindersley:** Natural History Museum, London (c). **marinethemes.com:** Kelvin Aitken (bl, bc); Saul Gonor (cl). **8–9 Dorling Kindersley:** Natural History Museum, London (c). **9 Corbis:** Jeffrey L Rotman (tr). **Dorling Kindersley:** Natural History Museum, London (bc). **marinethemes.com:** Kelvin Aitken (br); Andy Murch (cl); Franco Banfi (bl). **10 marinethemes.com:** Kelvin Aitken (b). **11 marinethemes.com:** Kelvin Aitken (tr, crb, br). **12 Corbis:** Douglas P Wilson / Frank Lane Picture Agency (cl, clb, bl). **13 Corbis:** Jeffrey L Rotman (t). **SeaPics.com:** Doug Perrine (b). **14 Alamy Images:** Dan Callister (b). **marinethemes.com:** Kelvin Aitken (ca). **15 Corbis:** Tom Brakefield (br). **Getty Images:** James Forte / National Geographic (tr); Jeff Rotman / Iconica (tc). **marinethemes.com:** Kelvin Aitken (c). **16–17 Corbis:** Clouds Hill Imaging Ltd.. **18 Getty Images:** Barcroft Media (br); Jonathan S Blair / National Geographic (bl). **marinethemes.com:** Kelvin Aitken (cr). **21 Getty Images:** Stephen Frink / The Image Bank (tr). **marinethemes.com:** Kelvin Aitken (tl). **SeaPics.com:** Doug Perrine (tc). **22 Alamy Images:** Mark Conlin (tl). **Dorling Kindersley:** The Trustees of the British Museum (c). **22–23 Getty Images:** Yoshikazu Tsuno / Afp (b). **23 SeaPics.com:** Doug Perrine (tr). **24 Dorling Kindersley:** Natural History Museum, London (cr). **26–27 Science Photo Library:** Christian Darkin. **28 Corbis:** Tim Davis. **29 marinethemes.com:** Andy Murch (bc). **30 Alamy Images:** Mark Conlin (bc). **marinethemes.com:** Saul Gonor (bl); Andy Murch (crb). **SeaPics.com:** Marty Snyderman (cl). **31 marinethemes.com:** Kelvin Aitken (cl, bc, c, tl). **ceanwideImages.com:** Bill Boyle (br). **32 marinethemes.com:** Kelvin Aitken (cr, tl, cl, bl). **33 Dorling Kindersley:** Jón Baldur Hlíðberg (www.fauna.is) (cl). **marinethemes.com:** Kelvin Aitken (tr, br). **34 marinethemes.com:** Kelvin Aitken (cl). **34–35 marinethemes.com:** Andy Murch (b). **35 marinethemes.com:** Kelvin Aitken (tr). **naturepl.com:** Ian Coleman (WAC) (tl). **36 marinethemes.com:** Kelvin Aitken (b). **37 marinethemes.com:** Kelvin Aitken (tl); Ken Hoppen (br). **OceanwideImages.com:** Rudie Kuiter (bl). **38 OceanwideImages.com:** Rudie Kuiter (b). **39 marinethemes.com:** Kelvin Aitken (tl). **www.uwp.no:** Erling Svenson (b). **40–41 OceanwideImages.com:** Rudie Kuiter (tl). **40 marinethemes.com:** Kelvin Aitken (b). **SeaPics.com:** Stephen Kajiura (tl). **41 marinethemes.com:** Kelvin Aitken (br); (clb). **42 naturepl.com:** Doug Perrine. **43 marinethemes.com:** Kelvin Aitken (t, b). **Photolibrary:** (bl). **44–45 OceanwideImages.com:** Rudie Kuiter (r). **46 Photolibrary:** (bl). **46–47 Corbis:** Norbert Wu / Science Faction (c). **47 Alamy Images:** WaterFrame (r). **48 SeaPics.com:** Kubo / e-Photography (cl). **48–49 marinethemes.com:** Kelvin Aitken (bc). **49 OceanwideImages.com:** Rudie Kuiter (br). **SeaPics.com:** Marty Sniderman (tr). **50 marinethemes.com:** Kelvin Aitken (tl, cl, bl); Andy Murch (br). **51 marinethemes.com:** Kelvin Aitken (t). **OceanwideImages.com:** Bill Boyle (b). **52–53 naturepl.com:** Alex Mustard. **54–55 Ecoscene:** Andy Murch (l). **55 SeaPics.com:** Mark Strickland (br). **56 marinethemes.com:** Mark Conlin (cl). **57 Dorling Kindersley:** Natural History Museum, London (tc). **marinethemes.com:** Kelvin Aitken (tl); Mark Conlin (tr). **58 marinethemes.com:** Kelvin Aitken (tr). **OceanwideImages.com:** David Fleetham (br). **SeaPics.com:** D R Schrichte (tl). **59 marinethemes.com:** Kelvin Aitken. **60 marinethemes.com:** Kelvin Aitken (tl, bl); Jez Tryner (cl). **OceanwideImages.com:** Rudie Kuiter (br). **61 Alamy Images:** Andy Murch / Vwpics (br). **OceanwideImages.com:** Rudie Kuiter (tr). **SeaPics.com:** Scott Michael (bl). **62–63 Getty Images:** Digital Vision / Justin Lewis (t). **62 marinethemes.com:** Mike Parry (bl). **63 Alamy Images:** Underwater Imaging (r). **64–65 Alamy Images:** Martin Strmiska. **66–67 Alamy Images:** Reinhard Dirscherl (c). **67 Alamy Images:** Kelvin Aitken / First Light (tr). **68–69 marinethemes.com:** Kelvin Aitken. **70. Naturepl.com:** Doug Perrine (t). **71 Alamy Images:** WaterFrame (bl). **72 SeaPics.com:** Lisa Collins (t). **73 SeaPics.com:** Scott Michael (b); D R Schrichte (t). **74 marinethemes.com:** Kelvin Aitken (cr); Mary Malloy (cl). **75 Dorling Kindersley:** Natural History Museum, London (tl). **marinethemes.com:** Kelvin Aitken (tc); Andy Murch (tr). **NHPA / Photoshot:** Franco Banfi (b). **76 SeaPics.com:** Stephen Kajiura (tl). **76–77 Ardea:** Gavin Parsons (r). **78–79 marinethemes.com:** Saul Gonor. **80–81 marinethemes.com:** Kelvin Aitken (b). **81 Corbis:** Jeffrey L Rotman (tr). **82–83 Dorling Kindersley:** Jeremy Hunt - modelmaker (c). **82 Alamy Images:** Doug Perrine (tl). **83 marinethemes.com:** Andy Murch (tr). **84–85 Alamy Images:** Dan Callister. **86 FLPA:** Norbert Wu / Minden Pictures (c). **87 marinethemes.com:** Kelvin Aitken (br, tl); David Fleetham (tr). **SeaPics.com:** Peter McMillan (cl); Scott Michael (tc). **88–89 OceanwideImages.com:** Rudie Kuiter (tc). **Photolibrary:** (bc). **88 marinethemes.com:** Ken Hoppen (cla). **89 naturepl.com:** Alex Mustard (br). **90–91 naturepl.com:** Florian Graner (tc). **90 SeaPics.com:** Doug Perrine (b). **92 naturepl.com:** Doug Perrine (bl). **92–93 marinethemes.com:** Kelvin Aitken (bc). **SeaPics.com:** Doug Perrine (t). **93 SeaPics.com:** Doug Perrine (bl). **94 marinethemes.com:** Andy Murch. **95 marinethemes.com:** Kelvin Aitken (b). **96–97 Getty Images:** Paul Kay / Oxford Scientific. **98 Alamy Images:** Mark Conlin (bl). **marinethemes.com:** Kelvin Aitken (cl). **101 marinethemes.com:** Kelvin Aitken (b). **OceanwideImages.com:** Rudie Kuiter (t). **102–103 Science Photo Library:** Jason Isley / Scubazoo (l). **103 Thomas Gloerfelt:** (br). **104–105 Getty Images:** Georgette Douwma / Digital Vision (bc). **marinethemes.com:** David Fleetham (tc). **105 Alamy Images:** WaterFrame (br). **106–107 Getty Images:** Alexander Safonov / Flickr. **108 Dorling Kindersley:** David Peart (b). **108–109 marinethemes.com:** Andy Murch (t). **109 Getty Images:** Rainer Schimpf / Gallo Images (b). **110 Dreamstime.com:** Ruben Martinez Barricarte (tl). **Getty Images:** James R D Scott / Flickr (bl). **110–111 Alamy Images:** Andy Murch / Vwpics (tc). **111 marinethemes.com:** Andy Murch (r). **112–113 marinethemes.com:** Andy Murch. **114 Getty Images:** Stephen Frink / Stone (tr). **arinethemes.com:** David Fleetham (b). **115 marinethemes.com:** Stephen Wong (b). **116 Corbis:** Norbert Wu / Science Faction (t). **Getty Images:** Jonathan Bird / Peter Arnold (b). **117 Corbis:** Andy Murch / Visuals Unlimited (bl). **Getty Images:** Gerard Soury / Oxford Scientific (tl). **SeaPics.com:** Stephen Kajiura (tr). **118–119 SeaPics.com:** Martin Strmiska. **120 Corbis:** Paul Souders. **121 marinethemes.com:** Kelvin Aitken (bc). **123 Corbis:** Norbert Wu / Science Faction (crb). **marinethemes.com:** Kelvin Aitken (tr). **124 marinethemes.com:** Kelvin Aitken (cl, br); Andy Murch (tl, bl). **125 FLPA:** Norbert Wu / Minden Pictures (b). **marinethemes.com:** Andy Murch (t). **126 OceanwideImages.com:** Andy Murch (bl). **126–127 Andy Murch / Elasmodiver.com:** (bc). **127 marinethemes.com:** Andy Murch (tc). **Robert Harding Picture Library:** Marevision / age fotostock (tr). **128 Getty Images:** Visuals Unlimited, Inc. / Andy Murch (bl). **130 Getty Images:** Bill Curtsinger / National Geographic (bl). **marinethemes.com:** Kelvin Aitken (cl). **130–131 marinethemes.com:** Kelvin Aitken (bc). **131 Getty Images:** Visuals Unlimited, Inc. / Andy Murch (br). **marinethemes.com:** Kelvin Aitken (tr). **132 marinethemes.com:** Andy Murch (b). **133 marinethemes.com:** Andy Murch (tl). **134–135 SuperStock:** age fotostock (l). **135 SeaPics.com:** Manfred Bail (tr). **136 marinethemes.com:** David Fleetham (cr). **137 Corbis:** Stephen Frink (cl). **SuperStock:** age fotostock (tr). **138 Getty Images:** Visuals Unlimited, Inc. / Andy Murch (cl, bl). **139 marinethemes.com:** Andy Murch (b). **SeaPics.com:** Mark Conlin (t). **140 Corbis:** Stephen Frink / Aurora Photos. **141 Alamy Images:** blickwinkel / Schmidbauer (b). **Getty Images:** Roger Munns - Scubazoo / Science Faction (t). **142–143 marinethemes.com:** Kelvin Aitken. **144 OceanwideImages.com:** Andy Murch (b). **145 marinethemes.com:** Kelvin Aitken (t, b).

Cover images: *Front:* **Dorling Kindersley:** Natural History Museum, London tl, cl, tc, clb, bc, cla, cb